11
DAYS
IN MAY

JD Messinger

Waterfront Digital Press

Waterfront Digital Press
2055 Oxford Avenue
Cardiff, CA 92007

First hardcover edition September 2012

For information about special discounts for bulk purchases, please con-
tact The Messinger Group, at www.JDMessinger.com

Library of Congress Cataloging-in-Publication Data is available

ISBN: 978-1-933754-93-2

Manufactured in the United States of America

For further information please visit

www.JDMessinger.com

www.WaterfrontDigitalPress.com

DEDICATION

This book is dedicated to my entire family, but especially my amazing daughter Madison, who taught me almost everything I know about writing; my patient wife Marianne, who I am nominating for sainthood; and my older sister Patricia, who is always my pointer. So they may understand and believe what I have come to see, feel, and know in every cell of my being. Perhaps it helps to explain that unusual experiences are not all that unusual. May you discover your essence and dare to disturb the universe.

"I want to know God's thoughts. The rest are details."
~ Albert Einstein

11 DAYS IN MAY

"JD Messinger is a remarkable, amazing person who has given voice to a truly unique message in *11 Days in May*. By confronting our need for control and our fear of letting go, JD's message creates renewal and hope. Indeed, learning to trust in ourselves can begin to change our world."

Stephen M. R. Covey, *The New York Times* and
1 *Wall Street Journal* bestselling author
of *The Speed of Trust* and co-author of *Smart Trust*

"The World of Form has dominated modern civilization and blinded us to the deeper reality that JD Messinger calls the World of Light. I call it the Akasha Dimension. I believe that it is the fundamental reality of the universe. The A-field, or World of Light, is the hidden dimension that spiritual cosmologies have always affirmed and it is now being rediscovered by science. We can all be grateful to JD for calling it to our attention in this warm, enticing, and highly readable series of conversations. Everyone who wants to know more about the "real" nature of reality would do well to read *11 Days*."

Dr. Ervin Laszlo, Founder of the Club of Budapest,
author of *Science and the Akashic Field*

"JD Messinger has produced a modern visionary spiritual classic that connects his experiences with the perennial philosophy that we are one with the Source of it all and need only grow in our awareness of that oneness to find true peace and joy. This is the story of a spiritual journey that a lot of people will be able to relate to and appreciate. The genre is unique and all JD. In the end, it is not about the love that has its beginnings in us, but about the Love in which we have our beginnings."

Dr. Stephen G. Post, President,
Institute for Research on Unlimited Love

"In *11 Days in May,* JD Messinger has crafted a thought-provoking and fascinating book, which investigates the myriad of ways in which all of reality is connected and interrelated. Many profoundly provocative insights will help us to better understand the fascinating milieu in which we live, which he has dissected and examined with a truly rare talent and skill. I highly recommend *11 Days* for any serious student of human destiny and its implications."

Miceal Ledwith, L.Ph., L.D., D.D., LL.D.,
Professor of Systematic Theology, Maynooth College,
Ireland, University President, and Member
of the International Theological Commission for 17 years

"Wow! No one is more uniquely qualified to speak of letting go of control than J D Messinger. This "out of the box" message is one that we all need to consider. I applaud JD for having the courage to express it so authentically. Contemplating life's deepest questions is a critical exercise that aids us in reaching our full potential. *11 Days in May* addresses the fear of letting go and embraces trust in a way that has never been done before. It delivers a message of hope and renewal for all those who have struggled with control. Read it and reflect."

Greg Link, Co-Author, *Smart Trust: Creating Prosperity,
Energy, and Joy in a Low-Trust World*

"*11 Days in May* is an evolutionary gold medal! As a former world gold medalist and Olympian, I know that to achieve greatness we must master the art of detachment and live the game moment-by-moment, practicing perfection in every breath. *11 Days* epitomizes the essence of the Olympic spirit—courage, dedication and passion—for the noble cause of restoring greatness while promoting peace and unity. If you're looking for an inspirational story that cuts across all realms of existence, your search is over!"

Daniel Lyons, World Gold Medalist, Pan American
Gold Medalist and 1988 Seoul Olympian

TABLE OF CONTENTS

ACKNOWLEDGMENTS

This book would not have been possible without the love, knowledge, and assistance of many people. This support has been manifested in two realms of our existence, physical and spiritual, and both are equally important—and the more I reflect—inseparable. I am especially grateful and would like to thank the following people:

My wife Marianne, daughters Madison and Taylor, son Grant, sister Patricia, and niece Kristen, for the spiritual bond we share as a soul family and for all the lessons you have shared and countless ways you have guided me through signs and synchronicities

The countless doctors, authors, philosophers, scientists, theologians, and healers who are far too numerous to list, for sharing their essence to help me discover, believe, and use my essence to fulfill my purpose

My agent, Bill Gladstone, for taking me under his wing and providing the knowledge and wisdom to make this book a reality

My amazing editors for their magic with words, structure, inspiration, and grammar; Yi Shun Lai, Madison Messinger, and Marianne Messinger

My cover designer, Barry Mack, for the fun and magic that unfolded before our eyes

My friends at the Morguelan Energy Institute for helping me to unleash all limiting thoughts and tap into the source energy for the purpose of love

My publicist, Imal Wagner, for her intuition, hard work, and the grace that emanates around her

My partners in the quest for truth who spent months debating the nature of life, living and our purpose for existence; Patricia McCrann, Bo Rinaldi, Jennifer Combs, and Joe Heller

Preface:

The Battlefield
Where We Now Stand

In the beginning, there was cosmic energy and there was silence. Source was the cosmic energy, and the cosmic energy was Source. And there was silence in no place, in no time.

Source created matter because Source wanted to share cosmic love. The non-physical matter evolved into physical matter and now there was a Place in no time. Still, there was silence.

Physical matter was graced with life force and species were created. Now there were creatures in the Place in no time, and the silence was over.

And the creatures gained intelligence, knowledge, and wisdom. Moreover, there was love amongst them for the land, air, water, and each other, and Source was pleased.

Then time and beliefs were formed, followed by weapons and money. Occasionally, the creatures disagreed. Yet, the creatures were few, the resources plentiful, and the leaders wise; therefore, Source remained satisfied.

The creatures multiplied, requiring an agricultural revolution. The few became many, and more disagreements arose. Yet, with a bounty of resources and wise leaders, the Place was secure, but Source took notice.

The many needed more, demanding an industrial revolution. Industries and institutions formed, the importance of time and money grew, fewer but larger battles ensued. The wise were challenged by a powerful few and lost influence. Still, the resources were sufficient. However, Source was concerned and planted Seedlings.

And scientific revolutions began and what once was dark became light. Global webs and networks connected the many, time and distance collapsed, and the Place became interdependent. The wise leaders were replaced by a powerful few, resources became scarce, and the Seedlings of Source grew in size and stature.

The powerful few became corrupt. Prudence, justice, temperance, and fortitude were discarded. Moral laws were violated, and what once was light became dark. The many became confused and were seduced into buying things they did not need and could not afford, all to ease their mental suffering. As material addictions grew, suffering transformed into physical pain. An unsustainable model was born with paper, chemicals, and electromagnetic waves that perpetuated the addictions.

The Seedlings offered warnings and divinely inspired solutions. Sweet-talking sirens, blinded by sense-filled pleasures and addicted to the World of Form, however, deafened the powerful few.

Wants outweighed needs, resources were squandered, life force abused, trust destroyed, all to please the senses and deaden the spirit, which expanded the darkness.

The imbalance reached a tipping point. Love of money and toys superseded love of cosmic gifts and life force. The new leaders lied. Accountability and responsibility were destroyed, and great illusions were perpetuated to sustain the artificial environment. Chaos was imminent, yet the new leaders remained blind and deaf.

Legions of knowledgeable Seedlings became messengers of Source. They formed global armies, bearers of light, to restore balance during the period of great change.

The unsustainable models and addictions will end. The essence of governments and industries, the essence of science and faith, and the essence of life and living will all change. A revolution has begun, divinely ordained to end the illusions and to restore balance and harmony.

Each must choose. Will it be toys or nature, self or the many, today or tomorrow, gratification or satisfaction?

It is a love story between whom and what we love more.

The conflict is between man and Source. The battlefield is between the mind and soul. The weapons are trillions of electrical impulses, the essence of every thought.

When the illusions are shattered the senseless consumption, material addictions, and abuse of the many will end.

It will end. Where, how, and when is up to man to decide.

This is where we now stand, and our thoughts are the enemy.

November 11, 2008
1840 Log Cabin
Austin, Texas

DEAR READER

I was living the high life when it happened: A C-suite executive with a life's worth of experience behind me and a wealthy existence all around, I couldn't possibly have predicted that my neck would break for the second time in my life.

But happen it did, in January 2000—and with the crushed discs and nerves went the glass barrier that had, until then, sheltered me from the meaning and purpose of life.

While in rehabilitation, I left my body, conversed with God, and experienced prophetic visions and powerful insights.

I desperately needed to know how and why I could experience what was happening to me—and, ultimately, I needed to know who I was. But how could I publicly admit my doubts and questions? I was a CEO at Ernst & Young consulting in Singapore, one of thirty-seven distinguished graduates from the United States Naval Academy class of 1981. I'd been a nuclear submarine officer and an advisor to cabinet officials. I could lose everything.

But I needed to know. I went on a quest that I hoped would answer my questions and save my sanity.

I interviewed hundreds of people, read thousands of research papers and hundreds of books. Eventually I launched a radio show to help find more answers and try to open a conversation about my questions. Ten years later, I still didn't have all the answers but I was slowly discovering them.

At the same time, I took sharp notice of our world: We're on the edge of an abyss. Each disaster eclipses the next. I am compelled to share the answer to the questions. I once asked, "Why now?" but the answer is as profound as it is simple: Never before have so few controlled so many, or so many had so little, or a global revolution been so close. We all must choose between whom and what we love more.

The parables in this story span 30 years. I share my story as it happened.

I want to help others believe what I came to accept with absolute certainty: Based on my own experiences, there are no accidents, no coincidences, and no such thing as luck. What may be perceived as a shock or surprise is predictable, and an outcome of a series of laws and forces that guide and direct all of life and reality. Even the laws of physics, fundamental and theoretical, are part of this great mystery. I have done my best to put these experiences, which I once thought beyond description, into words.

One day near the end of my quest, I had a revelation that aided me in understanding my fears and helped me gain the courage to share these true events. I was reading *The Only Thing* by Bill McKenna. I read a chapter that explained that the opposite of love was not hate, but fear.

On a sheet of paper I listed my fears of sharing my story. I then wrote all the reasons I loved telling the facts: I love sharing knowledge and wisdom, helping other people, and promoting unity over division. I also love that truth is authentic, transparent, filled with adventure, and has the potential to increase faith and trust. I stared at the list and that was when the revelation struck me.

The fears were all about me; my reputation, my money and my life. Then I recognized that the love was about you; your peace, your understanding and your happiness.

I stared at my list, *how ironic*, I thought. *God gave me these words about making a choice, between self or others, gratification or satisfaction, and I haven't committed. I'm a damn hypocrite. A fake. If I don't tell this story, I'm a fraud.*

Then I remembered something about courage. Being courageous doesn't mean you aren't afraid. Courage means you are afraid, but you sail forward anyway and ignore the fear and potential storms.

I woke up. Again. I accepted that it wasn't about me; it's about serving others, restoring greatness and shattering the illusions that controlled my life and possibly yours. This was three years after I wrote the words that are now the Preface.

I decided it was about time to put my selfish, egotistical wants aside, and finally embrace those divinely inspired words, and to publish my story for country, God, and unity.

After five months of writing, the end was in sight. Sadly, I was losing steam and faith, as the fear returned. Was it really almost complete? Did I finally have it right? Would my work be accepted?

So many questions, but then again, that was the essence of my quest, to find answers to the great questions. Who knew it would take me so long? I was nearly crushed pursuing this crazy pipe dream. Like Hercules, every time I thought I had decapitated the Hydra, two more heads appeared. Before I knew it, I was lost in a tangle of snapping vipers: Physicists and priests, psychologists and biologists, philosophers and investors, all ready to bite if I made so much as the smallest misstep. Life can certainly get ugly, and fast.

I needed guidance. I didn't want it, I needed it, and there is a big difference. But to whom could I turn? As the light in the tunnel became dim, there was only one person I could think of, my dear, life long friend who I had not spoken with in many years. I called out to him immediately, and we met for eleven days in May. The following story is a compilation of my many questions, and the conversation that ensued—and the answers I received.

JD Messinger

Day One —

Inspiration, Thoughts and Intentions

Who Makes Things?

I would like to know who makes things. What I mean is, does God make all the trees, cars, and inventions or does man make them?

What prompts such a deep thought?

I know this may sound unbelievable, but I keep having these dreams and visions where I see things. Then, months later, in real life, I make them, and they turn out close to what I envisioned in my dream.

Would you mind sharing one?

In one dream, I saw blue sheets running through a large printing press. It stretched for perhaps a hundred feet. The blue sheets had a circular design on it, and the design had three wings. The press kept going *ka chunk, ka chunk, ka chunk, ka chunk, ka chunk, ka, ka chunk, ka chunk, ka!* The dream repeated every night for nearly seven days…and it drove me crazy!

Did you ever determine what it was?

Of course, that's why I want to know who makes things. It was a game, and the design was the logo of my company. I never even thought about the company until months after the dream.

That's not so odd, people often dream about work.

That might be true, if this was work. It was the dream that inspired me to make these things and it had nothing to do with my job at the time!

Many of the most famous inventors, creators, and writers have experienced these kinds of insights. Nicolai Tesla had visions of the alternating current motor for a decade, and Walt Disney saw the vision of EPCOT in his ceiling.

That's exactly what I mean! When I had my radio show, I interviewed many creative people who said the same thing. During one interview, a renowned artist told me that he had no idea what he was painting, it was unfolding before him as he had the brush in his hands. Once, just like Walt Disney, he said he saw it in his ceiling. So, back to the question: Who makes things?

That depends.

What does it depend on?

It depends upon what you believe God is.

Does God have arms and legs? Does he walk and talk amongst us? If not, then clearly it is man that makes things.

If God has arms and legs, must they not be the largest arms and legs, and if so, might these extremities take up the entire domain of the planet itself?

Clearly to be God, He must have very large arms and legs. How else could He make the planet?

Yet, God made more than just the planet. Did God not make the universe as well?

I see your point. Clearly, God must not have arms and legs for they would certainly have to be larger than the universe.

So then, you believe that man makes all the physical things on the planet.

It must be so; we just agreed that God couldn't possibly have arms and legs.

Really? Is that what we agreed or is that what you assumed?

Again, you are correct. I wrongfully assumed that you agreed with my logic.

Is this not the essence of what we are discussing, assumptions?

Excellent point. This is of course the purpose of me asking you these questions, to understand the essence of what it all means. I make so many assumptions everyday I fail to see them. Can you help me see what assumption I made?

You first assumed, correctly, I might add, that we agreed that the arms and legs of God would indeed have to be larger than the universe itself.

Oh, good. I'm glad you agree with me, otherwise, I would be very confused.

You then assumed, wrongly so, that because his arms must be so large, that I agreed with you that He must not have arms and legs.

I did make this assumption.

You then assumed your initial conclusion must be true, that man makes things.

Absolutely, what other possible explanation could there be?

Yes, clearly this must be so, for it is the hand of man that swings the hammer, the ingenuity of man that forges the nail, the creativity of man that designs the blueprints.

When you put it this way, you make me pause.

What makes you reconsider?

Now I wonder what it means to be the maker.

Is another assumption revealing itself?

It may very well be the hand that pounds the nail belongs to man, for this is physical, but these thoughts and ideas, what you spoke of as designs and blueprints, these did not require hands.

Did it not require hands to lay onto paper the concepts that created the blueprints?

Paper? You show your age and make me laugh; who uses such crude instruments today? It is all bits and bytes, digital; nothing is on paper now. But you seem to miss my point entirely.

Please explain.

I questioned what it was to make, the essence of making, if you will. It may have been the hands that drove the nail, but this is only the end of the making process. The process of making these things began long before.

It was the idea that first gave birth to every creation. Is this what you mean?

Precisely! At last, we agree.

Moreover, these ideas did not require arms and legs.

Hallelujah! By golly, we are finally getting somewhere.

Are we now back to God being the source of all things made?

Yes, I do believe we have resolved this. God is the maker of all.

Does the final stage of making still require the hammer?

It must.

Which only man can yield since God has no extremities?

Oh my. Must we bring this back up again?

Did you or did you not ask me to help you answer the question?

Yes, I did.

Do you wish to resolve it today?

I couldn't stand verbal gymnastics on this one more day. Let's finish it now. Who holds the hammer?

Why man of course. Who brought forth the idea?

God! It must be God! I will not debate this again!

What then is the maker of things?

You and your ways; if this weren't so important to me I would have ended this conversation long ago. Fine, have it your way. Besides, I'm in a hurry you know. Clearly, it must be both man and God.

You speak as if they are separate and distinct.

Of course they are separate. How preposterous! To propose otherwise would be blasphemy.

Are you making another assumption?

No, this is not an assumption. Of this, I am certain. If it were an assumption that would mean that my parents, teachers, and pastor are all wrong.

Then how did the idea from God, get into the hands of man?

I don't know the answer to that. Only God knows that.

Did God use one of those old letters and a stamp?

That is not funny.

Perhaps He sent an email or a text message?

No hands and arms means no fingers as well. Honestly, you can be irritating.

How then did God share the idea?

A thought? Yes, it must have been a thought since thoughts do not require hands. There. Are you satisfied?

If God sends man a thought, and man executes the plans, which then is the maker?

Oh, well, as much as my ego hates to admit it, you might have a point. Let me think for a moment.

Take your time.

If the idea comes from God but requires the hands of man, then reluctantly I must admit that the maker of things must be a combination of the will of God and the execution of man.

This brings us back to your very first question.

My brain is so confused I can't remember. What was my initial question?

You asked me if God made things or if man made things.

Oh yes, I remember now.

You made another assumption.

I seem to be doing that a lot lately. Let me see, an assumption…Aha, I have it! I thought that man and God were separate and distinct beings.

Not just separate and distinct beings. What else did you assume?

Another assumption? Such a simple question and I made what, five assumptions?

Actually, it was closer to seven.

Seven assumptions, what were they?

You made two assumptions about what we agreed upon, another one or two about God's extremities, another on what it meant to make things, then you assumed God was the maker, reversed your assumption and said it was man, and then this last one about them being separate and distinct.

Is that it or is there more?

There is one more.

This is a real brain twister. I have to think about it…okay, I did and I have no idea. What else did I assume?

When you assumed that God and man were separate beings, you also assumed that the thoughts of one were not connected to the hands of the other.

~~~

WHAT IS A THOUGHT?

This last discussion on who or what made things and the idea that the hands of man are somehow connected to the thoughts of God raises another very important question. If our thoughts are inseparable, what exactly is a thought?

You just had one and you don't know?

I know what my thought was, but I don't know exactly what it is!

I am trying not to laugh. I am composed now. How are you going to find out?

I am asking you.

I am not going to do your thinking for you.

I am not asking you to think for me, I am asking you to help me understand my thoughts.

Why do you want to know?

Come on, the implications are profound. Did God put the thought in my head about making a game, and creating a company? If so, which thoughts are mine? Do you see my dilemma?

Indeed I do.

I really need to understand this whole subject of thoughts. What is a thought and how can God put a thought in my head?

Begin by understanding the difference between thinking and thoughts.

Do you always talk in circles? What did you just ask me?

Is there a difference between the verb "to think," and the noun "a thought"?

All I know is that thinking about how and what I think is very confusing. In fact, I believe that if I try to think about my thoughts, my thoughts will change. Then I will lose track of what I am thinking about! You see it's an endless loop, the results will be uncertain! Now I'm making myself dizzy.

Try harder. I will wait.

All right then; I believe that "thinking" is the process my brain uses to develop a thought. The "thought" is the result of a thinking process. I believe that was perfect, but don't ask me to say it again, 'cause I think I forgot it already.

This is partially correct. Some thoughts are a result of your thinking, but others are transmitted to you. We said that when we discussed who makes things.

That's why I want to understand what a thought is so I can understand how others transmit them.

What are movies, books, commercials, the Internet, television, and music?

They are all thoughts in different media but that generates a question.

Proceed.

How could I stop others from transmitting thoughts to me? For example, sometimes I really don't like what is in the paper, on the news or on television. What am I supposed to do, cover my ears?

You need to stop listening to their words or watching their pictures.

Even when I do, the thoughts are still there, in my head.

Go spend time in nature, or in the water, such as a pool, shower, or the ocean. It helps to clear your mind and find your own thoughts.

How does water stop a thought from being transmitted?

The essence of a thought is an electrical impulse. Water is very dense and it provides a natural shield.

I learned that on a submarine. We used a foot of water as a shield around the nuclear reactors to reduce the radiation from getting into the living and working compartments. I never thought about applying water to block or cleanse thought waves. However, I still find it hard to accept that others transmit thoughts to me. It sounds like voodoo, curses, or witchcraft.

Do you have a mobile phone?

I do.

Can your phone send and receive pictures, music, and documents?

Of course! What a silly question.

Of what materials are those emails and pictures made?

They are packets of digital information.

Put on your nuclear engineering and math hat and tell me: What is the essence of this digital information?

Digital information is as its name states, information that is in the form of digits, numbers, what we call bits and bytes, or binary language.

How are these packets of numbers transmitted?

I see where you are going. The numbers are transformed into frequencies, and electrical impulses. In other words, the essence of all those documents, books, and movies are photons.

Of course, that is why they are sent around the world in fiber "optic" cables. They are beams of light. Now tell me, how much more powerful than your mobile phone's computer is the supercomputer sitting on your shoulders?

I have no idea, but I am sure it is millions of times more powerful.

Would you believe billions or possibly trillions of times more powerful?

Yes, I can believe that. The most powerful supercomputers in the world cannot even come close to replicating the power of the human brain, so a mobile phone has to have an infinitesimally small ability compared to my brain. So what you're telling me is that my thoughts are no different than the information on my phone. They are both electrical impulses.

That is correct. Are you satisfied? Have we answered your question?

Maybe we answered my initial question, but now I have more!

Of course you do. You want to know where thoughts are stored, how others send them, how God can send them, and perhaps you want to know how you can send thoughts to others. Am I correct?

I think you read my mind.

Did I read your mind or did your mind send the thought and I "translated" it using my supercomputer?

I have no idea exactly who is doing the sending or receiving, but I am now completely aware that is it taking place.

Did you come up with that idea yourself, or was it placed there?

If this keeps up much longer, I will have to jump into the ocean.

Witty. You always did have a great sense of humor.

I thought that was rather good, thank you.

Allow me to ask a simple question.

Fire away.

What is your brain?

I'm not a doctor and I'm afraid if I try to answer that, I might make a lot more then seven incorrect assumptions, which I am sure you will point out.

Does your brain have a power adapter? By this I mean a receptacle where you plug it in.

I believe we call that food, and the energy comes from carbohydrates, fats, and proteins that go through a chemical process in the mitochondria but that's all I know.

Good enough. Does your brain have a data bank, or storage repository, like a computer's hard drive, where information is stored?

If it did, I suspect it would have set off the metal detector at the airport.

You are correct. There is no hard drive in your head. Every thought, memory or image is stored in your energy field. Having said that, is it okay with you if we simplify this discussion by saying that your brain is the computer that is doing not only the "thinking" process, but also the sending and receiving?

I'm fine with that. It reminds me of my days on a submarine with our sonar system. We could listen with our receivers or send with our transducers. Therefore, my brain is a giant transducer and receiver of information.

Are we in agreement that the essence of a thought is a photon and that your processor generates some thoughts but others are placed there?

I agree with that.

What do you recall from our discussion on what makes things?

I distinctly remember that I thought man and God were separate and distinct beings. We agreed they weren't, and we also agreed that the thoughts of one are inseparable from the hands of the other.

Indeed, the thoughts and actions of one do influence the behaviors and thoughts of another.

Hold on, I just had a thought.

What was it?

Perhaps it is more accurate to say a realization.

That is even better.

What you just shared with me, and I with you, that means that all of our thoughts, human and divine, are flying about together, carrying information and knowledge. The implication is that people are a collective thought sharing machine.

You have realized a great secret of the universe.

So where does this leave me?

You know what thoughts are, and where they come from, how they are transmitted, and that your brain is a sender and receiver of these thoughts. However, you do not know where they are stored.

I'm thinking.

I can tell.

Why does a thought need to be stored anywhere?

Excellent question. Why indeed?

It is not something we can touch. It isn't like a box of cookies that needs to be stored in the pantry. It's amorphous, non-physical, and always changing. Now I understand why you said memories are stored in my energy field.

It doesn't require food or water; it never dies; it contains information and travels around the world in well under one second and it can go on and on and on forever.

I just had what I think is another insightful thought.

I like profound thoughts.

If I am a collective thought generating and sharing machine, then why am I not always aware of these thoughts? What I mean is, sometimes I am able to receive thoughts, but sometimes I'm not. That's pretty amazing.

It certainly is.

It occurred to me when you said it doesn't require food or water.

Why is that?

I'm hungry.

What does that have to do with anything?

Thoughts, and the associated knowledge and information, must exist for all eternity.

They do.

Since I am so hungry, and these thoughts exist for all eternity, that means I can stop thinking for now and pick this up again after I eat?

You most certainly may.

~~~

WHAT ARE INTENTIONS?

Now that I have recharged my system, I want to pick up from my last thought. Surely, there are trillions upon trillions of knowledge packets flying around me every one billionth of a second in the form of thoughts, radio and television signals and mobile devices. Why then is it that sometimes my receiver picks up these thoughts and other times it doesn't?

Your receiver is always picking them up, but you are discarding them.

Discarding them? Why would I want to discard them?

It has to do with your intentions.

Although I did a radio interview on intentions, I never really asked myself exactly what an intention is?

Intentions are the precursors to thoughts.

How can there be a thought before a thought?

I didn't say it wasn't a thought. It is, but it is a different kind of thought.

What is the difference between them?

Tell me what we said a thought was.

We said a thought was the result of the thinking process and that it was photons filled with information and knowledge.

Would you agree that there are different kinds of thoughts?

Do you mean good thoughts and not-good thoughts?

That is one way to categorize thoughts but I was referring to the kinds of thoughts you have. Give me an example of some thoughts you have throughout your day.

I suppose prayers might be one kind. Oh, here's another kind: Hopes and dreams.

Carry on.

I'm trying, but I'm not sure there are many more.

What distinguishes these different types of thoughts?

I guess that would be the goal.

The goal?

The reason I'm having that thought.

Is it safe to say the objective of all thoughts is to resolve a problem or achieve a goal?

I think that is an excellent beginning, yes.

Why do you say beginning?

I don't know. It just popped out of me.

By that, you mean you cannot rationally explain the source of that thought.

I just said it. I don't know why.

Those are powerful.

What is powerful?

A thought that comes to you without having to think about it is the most powerful thought.

What kind of thought is that?

Inspired thoughts.

What is the source of an inspired thought?

If it did not come from your mind, where might it have come from?

It must have been floating around me, and my receiver picked it up.

Why would that be?

My goodness, we're going in circles! That's what I'm asking *you*! Why is it that sometimes my receiver gets it and other times it doesn't?

I told you before, but you were too busy thinking. You shut down your receiver.

What did you tell me?

I told you that you are always receiving information and inspired thoughts but you are not always paying attention. The answer to your question—why you receive some thoughts and not others—is your intentions. If your conscious intention is to solve a problem or achieve a goal your receiver picks up the answer. It is similar to when you are thinking about buying a yellow Volkswagen beetle and all of a sudden you start to see them everywhere. You set your intention to see them. It was the first thought.

Oh my, I see! I was trying to solve a problem and I got an answer!...Uh oh.

What's the matter now?

I forgot where we were.

You really must clear your mind and be present, in the moment. You said the inspiration you had was giving you the answer to the problem without you having to think about it. You were trying to identify what an intention is, and you said that intentions are the BEGINNING of the thought process.

This is like a math postulate.

What is a postulate?

It's an if-then statement. If all thoughts are to achieve a goal or solve a problem, then the first thought in the thinking process is establishing the intention.

That is correct. You receive the thoughts and inspirations when you set an intention. Now let me ask you this, isn't solving a problem a goal in and of itself?

Yes it is. Perhaps we can simplify it by saying that all thoughts are a result of an intention to achieve a goal.

The simpler we can make it the better. What we now know is that the intention is the beginning of the thought process and therefore, it is the motivation behind the conscious thought. The interesting part is that although your thought is conscious, the intentions are sometimes not.

That makes sense and that is exactly what just happened! I was motivated to understand what an intention is; I set an intention to understand an intention, and I got the answer! An intention is the *beginning* of the thought process.

You said you were motivated. Do intentions have motivations?

All intentions have a motivation. There is a desire for an outcome, is there not?

Yes, I think you're right. There must be motivations behind intentions. Can you give me an example of a motivation?

Well, if my thought is about a dream then my motivation is that I want to make my dream come true!

Why?

It might be for fun or it could be to make money.

Give me another example. What about a prayer?

I don't know for sure, but I would presume that most of the time the motivation behind a prayer is from people who are in pain or suffering and they want help.

What if you're not in pain or suffering but are praying? What else might you be praying about?

If that is the case, I don't think you are praying *for* something. I think you are praying to *give* something, like thanks.

What would that be called?

Gratitude.

I do believe you understand intentions.

I do?

Indeed. Whether it is praying or dreaming, the underlying motivation behind all intentions is either a fear or a desire. Every thought has its root with one of these two motivations and this first thought is the intention, the beginning of the thought process that tunes your receiver to pick up information that helps you achieve your goal. Are we finished?

I have to think of it like the sonar system. If I wish to hear a whale, I look for one specific frequency, but if I am listening for an enemy submarine, it's another. I tune out the whale when I'm looking for the enemy.

I believe you have it.

Have it? I don't think I have it. I still don't understand why I received the signals for my game and company logo?

You wanted to leave your old job and start something new. You were not consciously aware of this intention. I said that before.

My goodness, you're right! At the time of the insights, I was not consciously aware that I was even thinking about starting a new company.

It was not rational.

No.

I'm getting old and forgetful, help me out. What did we call the source of an idea that was not rational?

It was an inspiration that was beyond me, outside my own mind.

I know, but what is beyond you?

The Divine.

Now you have it.

My goodness, a divine inspiration unconsciously helped me when I needed it most.

Why do you say when you needed it most?

I was in a lot of pain and really suffering. Well, that raises another series of excellent questions. I needed help because I was in a lot of pain and suffering. What is pain and suffering?

I think that is enough for one day.

Day Two —

PAIN, SUFFERING AND CONFUSION

WHAT IS PAIN?

I must share a significant and painful time in my life.

Pain is a part of the journey. Tell me what happened.

In 1985 I was a submarine officer. My ballistic missile submarine was being overhauled in the shipyard. One foggy night, I had an accident while on a routine check. A beam smashed into my head and snapped my neck.

That's terrible.

It was unbearable. I was in traction for a long time. I was given prescription painkillers, but they destroyed my stomach. So they gave me an electrical stimulation device. A battery pack on my hip sent electrical signals to four pads that were stuck to the pressure points on my upper back. Whenever the pain became too much to bear I cranked up the juice. The electrical signal was supposed to reduce the pain, but it didn't work too well.

You look fine now. I take it that you eventually overcame this problem.

True, I was in pretty good shape for almost fifteen years, but by the summer of 1999, my neck started to deteriorate again. I knew something was wrong since the pain returned and it was worse than before. By this time I was busy climbing the corporate ladder, so I just took Motrin. I was supposed to take one pill every four to six hours but by the time January 2000 came around, the pain was so bad that I was taking four every two hours. I wasn't really aware that I was consuming an entire bottle in less than a week.

I see. What happened next?

One morning I woke up and got out of bed. It seemed just like any other morning, but the events that unfolded forever changed my life. I walked to the bathroom and turned on the shower to let the water get hot. While I was waiting, I took off my pajamas, intertwined my fingers, and raised my arms for a nice morning stretch. That's when it happened. It felt like a six-inch axe was trying to split me in half. It sliced between my shoulder blades. I found out later that my collapsing vertebrae were crushing my nerves. I buckled over, but that hurt like crazy too. I snapped up and whipped back, screaming. The ruthless axe swung again and again. Ten thousand volts electrified every nerve in my arms and back. My own screams hammered at my eardrums. I staggered out of the bathroom screeching and reaching, my arms over my head as I tried to pull the axe out. My wife came running to my rescue. By now the screaming was existential, I was out of my body. I watched my wife, Marianne, try to catch my body as I—perhaps I should say it—collapsed. Its head hit the corner of the bedroom dresser then it flopped down to the floor like a rag doll.

What do you mean?

I left my body. I was watching it all happen like a movie.

How fascinating, an OBE, out of body experience. How long were you out of your body?

It wasn't a long time, perhaps a minute.

What happened next?

The nerves that worked my arms were crushed. They took bone out of my hip to put my neck back together. In the process of doing that, they had to move my trachea out of the way and cut through the nerves in my neck. I spent months learning how walk and talk and chew gum again.

Why did you do this to yourself?

Excuse me?

This neck incident, why did it happen?

It was an accident, there's no reason.

Really? Didn't we just have a discussion yesterday about intentions and thoughts?

What does that have to do with anything?

Why did this happen?

I told you. It was an accident.

Let me see if I have this right: When you send an intention to make your dreams come true, something wonderful happens. But when you refuse to see a doctor and crush the nerves in your neck, it's an accident.

Yes, yes it is.

Hmm.

What are you hmming about?

The weather.

What does the weather have to do with any of this?

It seems to be foggy on your side.

Oh really, is it now? Are you trying to say that I did this to myself with some hidden intention? That's preposterous! Why would I inflict unimaginable pain upon my own body? How does that make any sense?

Really, makes no sense? At the time you first injured your neck, in 1985, did you enjoy being on the submarine?

...

Hello, did you hear me?

I heard you.

Touch a nerve, did I?

That's not funny.

I did, didn't I?

Yes, you did. I hated the submarines. Well, not the submarines themselves, but the missiles. The idea of launching nuclear missiles made me sick to my stomach. I loved the Navy but not the idea of global annihilation.

I'm sorry. That must have been a difficult time. Why didn't you just leave the Navy?

I couldn't just leave. I had to serve my time.

Then you left the Navy, joined the corporate world, and worked your way up the corporate ladder. I'm sure that was much better.

It was, at least for a while.

Only a while?

I was living on a plane. Sometimes I made eight stops in four continents over ten days.

I take it you didn't like this.

No, I did not. It dragged me away from my children. And when I was home all I wanted to do was sleep. That didn't make my family too happy.

Is it possible then that the second time you injured your neck, while you were in the corporate world, was for the same reasons as the first time on the submarine? It was a subconscious and graceful way of getting out of a situation you didn't like.

Where exactly is this going? You are wearing my patience thin.

Patience, ah yes, a virtue meaning to be tolerant and understanding.

I am trying to understand, which is why I am asking so many questions.

I thought people asked questions when they didn't believe or didn't agree?

Sometimes they ask when they wish to understand.

What is it that you seek to understand?

I want to understand why I would inflict pain upon myself. Why did it happen? Was there some kind of lesson for me in this?

Now you're asking the proper question. You need to escape this denial.

Denial! Now I am stuck in denial. Exactly what am I denying?

You are denying that you did this to yourself, that your subconscious motivation was to leave the navy and then leave a company you didn't enjoy. You sabotaged yourself so that you could escape an environment you didn't want to be in. You did it twice.

I'm sorry, but I absolutely cannot accept that this is the reason for my pain. I refuse to believe that pain is a self-inflicted, hidden intention to subject myself to torture because I didn't have the guts to leave.

I'm sorry if I confused you, but what you just said is not pain.

What do you mean, not pain? Of course it was pain.

No, the essence of pain is the result of damaging a physical body. Nothing more.

If we haven't been talking about pain, what have we been talking about?

What you felt from damaging your body was pain. But the self-inflicted mental anguish that subconsciously created this incident is not pain.

If that's not pain then what is it?

The precursor to the pain was suffering. Suffering is mental, not physical.

~~~

WHAT IS SUFFERING?

Clearly, I have no idea what the difference is between pain and suffering.

I told you, pain is the result of having a physical body that occasionally is damaged.

Is pain accidental?

There are no accidents.

No accidents? The tree that falls on the house, the man who is hit by a car, the child who falls off a curb, and the fuse that melts and causes a fire. None of these are accidents?

What do you mean by an accident?

An accident is an incident where someone or something is damaged and it was not intentional.

Not intentional, like your neck.

Like my neck!

You are absolutely correct. How terrible of me to confuse the ability of your mind to create two different outcomes in your life.

What two outcomes?

The ability of your subconscious supercomputer to create a positive outcome, like forming a company, and the subconscious actions that caused you to ignore going to the doctor when your neck was falling apart. Clearly, there is no connection.

None whatsoever! What could possibly be the connection?

I have no idea.

Why do I have the sense that you do?

Perhaps it is a sixth sense, I do not know.

I don't believe in sixth senses.

That is the first thing you said today with which I completely agree; you do not believe in a sixth sense.

We have a consensus, how inspiring.

I did not say I didn't believe in a sixth sense, I said you do not believe in it and I agreed with you—that you do not believe in a sixth sense. Nevertheless, you had a sense. What exactly is that, a sense, some deep intuitive knowing without rational explanation? Might it possibly be a few million of your trillions of cells sending up a flare?

I don't know and I honestly can say I don't care.

Really, you don't care? Then who or what brought you to me, now? Why are you here asking all these questions? Why are you subjecting yourself to this torture and haranguing?

That's it! I don't have to take this. I have no idea why I sought your advice.

Are you in pain?

No, of course I am not in pain.

Are you upset?

Yes, I am very upset!

I'm sorry, was it something you ate?

No, it was not something I ate. It was you.

Me, something I ate? Not likely.

It has nothing to do with food you fool.

Then are you unhappy?

Yes, of course I am unhappy. I said that already.

There must be something wrong with my hearing, because I thought you said you were upset.

Upset, unhappy, who cares, what's the difference?

There is a huge difference, and since we have determined that it has nothing to do with food we should continue to seek to understand the source of your unhappiness.

I will save you the time and trouble: You accused me of inflicting pain on myself. This is why I am not happy.

No I didn't.

How can you say that? I heard you!

I said you were suffering.

There you go again, you're like a broken record. Pain, suffering; there's a difference. Upset, unhappy; there's a difference. What's the difference?

I told you, pain is the result of having a physical body that is damaged. Suffering is a condition created in the mind when the external environment is not consistent with the internal desire.

Say that again?

Suffering is optional and is created by the mind.

Why would I willingly choose to suffer?

Will is within your conscious mind. You don't willingly choose to suffer, it is not conscious. Suffering is subconscious, your internal rudder is screaming at you, demanding that you turn left, but your mind is insisting on going right.

You're confusing the hell out of me. Stop it!

Aha, you found it!

What did I find?

The source of suffering and unhappiness! It was another non-rational thought! My goodness, they are just popping out of you left and right.

What?

Confusion! Oh, this is wonderful!

Confusion is wonderful? Why is it wonderful?

No, no, you're confused.

That much I follow.

What is wonderful is that you found the source of your suffering and unhappiness!

What?

Confusion.

Why am I reminded of Abbot and Costello? Okay, I give up. What was I confused about?

You were clinging to something temporary.

What was I clinging to?

An outdated belief sometimes called an attachment.

What is an attachment?

An attachment is a form of mental virus. It is an object that the mind desperately wants but the body and soul usually do not need that comes from the World of Form.

A mental virus, how absurd!

These attachments were splitting you in half. Remember the axe you mentioned? Don't you see? The mind was probably attached to money, power or stock options. Really, you must pay more attention to the words that come out of your own mouth.

I am, at the present moment, quite conscious of the words coming out of my mouth. It is everything I can do to refrain from most of them being four-letter words.

Your soul was desperately trying to follow your heart and your dreams but your mind was not listening. The soul was pulling you forward to a happier and more joyful tomorrow but the mind was holding you back.

What was holding me back?

I told you, a mental virus called attachments and desires that only feed the mind. It could be any object that fuels lust, greed, power, or control.

Does Microsoft know about it yet?

It's in your brain computer, not in your laptop computer!

I have a malicious virus in my head?

Yes! Yes! Now you've got it. The source of your suffering and unhappiness is something that your mind is clinging to. It is attached to this object, a fixation. Do you see?

Argh!! Riddles, you're talking in circles. I am like a blind carpenter, clutching for tools; you say I see, but all I know is what I saw.

Let's begin with your confusion; we'll get to programs later.

Hold on a second! You're telling me that suffering is a condition created by being confused. Did I get that right?

Yes, you did. And it's optional; you don't have to suffer unless you want to. Unlike physical pain, suffering is a choice.

Okay, fine. If I did this to myself I'm pissed. Let's move on.

〜〜〜

WHAT IS CONFUSION?

Okay, let's get this over with. What was I confused about?

I don't know. You'll have to tell me.

If I was confused, how could I possibly know?

You know because it is behind you. Your higher self knows. Take a few deep breaths, and go inside. The answer is within.

I sense you are correct, but I'm not sure I can do what you suggest and figure it out by myself. It is clearly subconscious. I cannot put my finger on it.

Tell me, what happened between the second time you broke your neck in 2000 and started up your own company in 2003? What did you do during those three years?

I discovered I wasn't happy.

How did you discover this?

When I was lying in bed, unable to move my head and shoulders or walk, my family came to sit by my bed and keep me company. They tried to cheer me up, but it backfired.

Why do you say that?

They showed me pictures of the trips to Australia and the Great Wall of China.

That sounds nice. Family vacations are always filled with fun memories.

I didn't go on either trip. I was too busy working.

Why were you working so hard?

That's what I was supposed to do! Work hard, make more money, and get more promotions. Well…that's what I thought I was supposed to do.

You thought you were supposed to live to work. Who or what gave you that idea?

Social norms, the American culture, Madison Avenue, Wall Street, financial advisors, television commercials…how many do you want me to name?

You are talking about the outer world, the world of substance, form, if you will. You were hiding behind it.

What do you mean by hiding behind it, behind what?

You were like a child playing trick-or-treat, hiding behind a social mask, pretending to be someone else so you could continue to play in the World of Form.

Please, no more riddles. Is this social mask what you mean by the World of Form?

The World of Form is your name, job title, the company you work for, and your political or religious preferences. It is where you live, the places you visit, and the things you buy. It is objects and positions. It is everything that your mind thought that mattered most in life and they are all temporary. These things mean nothing to a soul, which is all we really are.

I'm not sure I completely follow the World of Form, but I do know that my job was my complete existence.

What happened to help you realize that this didn't make you happy?

I read five-dozen books on happiness, health, spirituality, money, success, and ancient wisdom. You name it; I read it.

Your soul was waking up. Was there any one book in particular that was more meaningful than the others?

You bet! It was *Self Matters*, by Dr. Phil McGraw.

Why was it so helpful?

I was on a search: I wanted to know who I was, why I was here and why I wasn't happy. The book helped me analyze all my critical choices, the defining moments in my life, and the people who influenced me.

What did you learn?

I discovered that every time I made a decision with love in mind, my life was balanced, happy and also successful. However, when I made choices in favor of security, prestige, wealth, or power, those decisions literally made me sick.

Can you give me an example?

The position as the CEO! I was very happy before that promotion, and I was also successful. However, my mind told me I needed to keep climbing the ladder, get more promotions, make more money, and earn stock options. It didn't end so well…remember the neck incident?

I remember. Is this about the time when you had your dream that lead to your games and new company?

Yes, the dreams and insights occurred during my time as CEO, shortly after I realized that I wasn't following my heart.

I see.

That's interesting.

What?

I never made the connection before.

What connection is that?

The one you made, or at least tried to help me see several times now.

Yes?

That an unconscious part of me was actually in charge of the ship! It must be my soul, spirit, higher self...use whatever name you want! My soul was trying to be my navigator, guiding and directing me toward a path that it knew was right for me. I never even knew it existed!

That's right, it was your soul. Because your mind was taking you off course, your soul took over. I told you that before. You were trapped in the World of Form. It was masking your inner self and your heart's desires. Your soul knew this.

If this course or life path was something I desperately wanted, why wasn't I paying attention? It doesn't make any sense to me.

This is the essence of confusion. It is a state of mind created from all the attachments and desires in the World of Form that are inconsistent with the desires and guidance of your soul. Your soul couldn't get through the mental interference...noise, attachments, advertisements and sweet talking sirens...from the World of Form, so your soul had to go into stealth mode.

Let me see if I have this right. My soul knew what was the right course, but my mind wanted to go somewhere else and my soul couldn't get through because of some kind of interference. Do I have that right?

Yes, you do. Think of the interference as anything that stops your soul from communicating with your mind. With one half of your essence wanting to go...say south, and the other half north, you become confused and don't know which way to turn. This confusion creates suffering, which ultimately leads to a physical pain.

I don't want my soul to call the axe man again. How do I stop the interference so all of my mental, physical and spiritual essence is heading in one direction?

You have to remove the programs from the World of Form I told you about. These not-good viruses are polluting your mental hard drive because they love playing with the attachments.

~~~

Day Three —

Programs, Values and Beliefs

What is a Program?

What exactly are these virus programs?

A program is a lens, a filter if you will, through which your senses perceive reality and then dictate your behavior. At the root of every program is a belief. Some programs are good and some are not-good. A virus program is not-good because it distorts the true nature of reality and creates unhealthy behaviors and habits. Another way of thinking about a program is like a software application on your desktop computer.

Who installed them?

Tell me what you know of your mind and how it works.

My mind has three major parts: The conscious, subconscious and unconscious. The conscious mind is the part that I am aware of, the part that is doing a task, aware of the television show, typing a document. It is the most limited part of the mind, meaning it can only manage a few tasks. Perhaps some people can manage seven, others ten, but it is a small number.

If you were to compare this to a laptop computer, what part of your computer would this be?

The RAM, the random access memory that is running the applications.

What happens if you try to run too many applications?

The applications go very slowly, or even lock up.

Very good, now tell me about the subconscious mind.

The subconscious mind is one layer deeper, just below the conscious. It is like the software applications installed on my computer. This part of my mind is a place where I install information, such as math, science, or driving directions. Once I install the software, it runs in the background without me having to think about it.

Excellent. What then is the unconscious mind doing?

The unconscious mind is like the operating system on a computer. It is sending trillions of impulses to a hundred trillion cells every fraction of a second. It keeps me walking, talking, and chewing gum.

What do you think would happen if everything that was taking place in your subconscious and unconscious mind were to become conscious? In other words, what if you could be aware of them?

I don't know for sure, but I suspect I would drop dead in a split second.

Why is that?

It would fry my brain! That's why we are unaware of the subconscious and unconscious.

Very good. Now, in what part of your brain has society installed values and beliefs?

I would say that's my subconscious mind, with the other software programs I learned.

That is correct. This is also where the programs that become the source of confusion reside. In order to prevent you from suffering, I have to help you recall them.

Isn't that what I did when I read all those books and did the exercises with Dr. Phil in *Self Matters*?

Exactly. Now, tell me, what did you discover that shocked you.

That's easy: I learned that I was working to live instead of living to work. Somewhere along my journey I became convinced that life was a destination at train station 401K in the city of retirement.

Anything else?

Yes, much more! I thought that money and promotions made me happy, and I realized they didn't! I also thought that the holy grail of life was something I could buy, sell or hold. So you think these beliefs are the root of the virus programs that confused me?

Indeed they are. These are the beliefs embedded in the program that defined your actions and behaviors. For example, the belief that the holy grail of life is something you can buy, created actions and behaviors to seek more promotions. These beliefs became the lens that pulled you deeper and deeper into the World of Form, which is not where your soul wanted to be.

I see. That's why you called these beliefs a virus, and the actions a not-good program that was destroying the plans of my soul. Okay, I get the idea of a software program, and a virus, and how it can be operating in the background without me knowing about it. Now I want to know how it got there without me realizing it.

Let me share a story. One day Mary asked Joanna to help her cook a pot roast. As she was preparing to put the roast in the pot, Mary told Joanna to cut the ends off. Joanna looked at the good meat and asked Mary to explain why she should cut off perfectly good, expensive meat. Mary replied that it's simply what her mother taught her. Joanna, recognizing the absurdity of cutting off good meat, pressed Mary to call her mother and ask why. Begrudgingly, Mary did so, only to have her mother reply, "I don't know. Why don't you ask your grandmother? She's the one who taught me." Mary called Grandma, and to her complete amazement, her grandmother replied, "You're cutting the ends off of perfectly good meat? Well dear, I don't know why you're doing it, but I did it because I had a small pot."

That's hysterical!

Why?

Because I totally get it! Everyone has family traditions, rituals, and cooking recipes, that are outdated. My dad, who grew up in the 1920s, thought that a woman's place was in the home, and no one was supposed to work on Sunday. I don't think many people believe those ideas anymore.

Where do these programs come from?

In the case of Mary, it came from her grandmother, who passed it down over sixty years.

Why did Joanna see the program?

Because she didn't grow up with Mary's mother and wasn't raised with that program. It didn't make sense to her, so she questioned it.

How did Mary respond?

Well, her immediate reaction was, "Just do it; that's the way it is."

Yet, Joanna persisted. Why?

She didn't want to waste expensive meat!

This is an example of an outdated program. Something that was valid and useful at one point in time, but not now.

What other kinds of programs are there?

There are also faulty programs, ones that you placed on your hard drive that were invalid to begin with. Can you think of any?

I sure can. While reading *Self Matters*, I was doing the exercises to discover defining moments, events that last a minute, but have such a huge impact that they create a program. When I relived this moment I found a subconscious program running and I had no idea it was installed!

Tell me about it.

One day, at six in the morning, I was getting ready to go to the airport. My wife came running out the front door. I looked up and she was wearing her pajamas. Something inside me started to boil. I jumped out of the car and shouted at her for being inappropriately dressed.

Why did you shout at her? What were you feeling?

She was embarrassing me in front of my driver, or so I thought at the time.

What happened next?

When I got into the car I was really angry! My blood was boiling, my ears were hot, my face flushed. I was mortified that Marianne had left the house in her pajamas. Then I realized it was a defining moment and it was like a punch in the gut. I saw how much I hurt her, the face I loved; the woman who traveled halfway around the world to be with me, gave birth to my children, this woman who's done nothing but love me. Basically, I felt like a real shit. That's when I began my deep yoga breathing and tried to go back into the moment, into the pain in my throat and the suitcase of emotions that was making every cell in my body tremble.

Then what?

Suddenly I saw an image. I was in my childhood home. I walked through the front door in the middle of the afternoon with my friends and I saw my mom. She was standing there in her pajamas and I was completely mortified! I could feel the stares of my friends burning holes in the back of my head.

What does this story reveal to you?

I was yelling at my wife, thirty-five years later, but it wasn't her I was yelling at; it was my mother. There she was standing in the hallway in the middle of the afternoon looking like a lazy bum in front of my friends! It made me feel incredibly ashamed.

Why did this happen, meaning, what caused this Mom-PJ program to kick in?

The way I see it, there had to be two things that took place at the same time. First, someone that represented my mother had to be in pajamas, and secondly, she had to be in front of someone who I felt would shame me.

Precisely! That kicked on the Mom-PJ "execute" switch in your subconscious mind. Now, tell me, how did the Mom-PJ program get installed in the first place?

I have actually thought about that a great deal, and again, I am not sure, but what I feel took place is that my system had a shock to it.

A shock? What do you mean?

I think of the program creation process like taking a picture. I was caught by surprise, by something that the child inside perceived as embarrassing, and my memory took a flash picture and stored that event and emotion in every cell of my being.

Is the Mom-PJ program gone now?

Actually yes, once my adult self discovered it lurking in the background I was able to delete it.

Wonderful! And how many of these faulty programs do you think you have installed in your memory bank?

I found dozens of them! One program was created when I was seven and my older brothers broke my Christmas present. That faulty program made me feel unloved at Christmas when my kids opened their presents. Another was installed when my parents left me with a mean uncle at age three and took the family to Florida without me.

What did that program say to you?

I wasn't loved enough to go on a family trip with everyone else. That one hurt.

Have we answered your first question? Have we defined what the programs are?

The programs are a collection of values and beliefs that are sitting in my subconscious mind. These beliefs dictate my behavior and essentially make me a programmed robot. Trigger the execute button and I am no longer in control of my behaviors. I'm sure there are thousands of them, and many of them are good. But some of them are outdated and others are faulty. Do I have it right?

Yes, you do. You need to remember that these programs dictate how you perceive reality and they influence all of your actions, behaviors, and thoughts. Whenever you are doing or saying something that deep inside you know is not you…there is a faulty or outdated program running.

That's a scary thought.

What's a scary thought?

The idea that I have hidden programs running that that are commanding all of my actions is scary! Just think, some of these might be a hundred years old!

I am sorry to say, but some of them are a couple thousand years old.

Wow. All I can say is wow.

Who or what installed these programs coercing you to work so hard? What about the one telling you that the purpose of life is to make money, go shopping, get more promotions, and then retire?

I don't know what to call it. It is sort of a conglomerate of external forces

Try.

I guess it would be the media, society, or maybe western culture.

It goes back long before the media existed.

How far back?

The "Original Download" goes back to the dawn of time.

The dawn of time, you mean like eight billion years ago?

I wasn't talking about the cliché; I was literally talking about the birth of time.

Time was born? I thought time existed forever.

Would that be a faulty or outdated program?

~~~

WHAT IS NOT-GOOD?

What is good?

My goodness, where did that question come from?

It was a thought, of course.

What prompted this deep thought?

I believe the programs that dictate what I think is good or bad are related to the root of my confusion. What I mean is that everyone is fighting to get my attention and money to support their cause, trying to convince me what I should value. No matter where I turn, people and the media say conflicting things. At least a third of the population says that abortion, democrats, sex, and gays are evil but they love money. Meanwhile another third says all those things are not evil but money is at the root of all this countries problems! As I reflect on our discussion about thoughts, it occurs to me that there could be a problem with my thinking.

How could there be a problem with your thinking?

Assume that every idea and invention is the will of God, implemented by the hand of man, and that God transmits nothing but good thoughts. How, then, do ideas become bad?

I understand your predicament. If your assumption about the will of God is true, there is a contradiction here.

Exactly. That's why I want to know what are good and evil, so society doesn't keep confusing me.

There is a truism that is helpful to remember in these situations.

What is that?

Whenever there appears to be a contradiction, you must reexamine your assumptions because at least one of them must be wrong.

Okay, I accept that. I remember how many assumptions I made when we talked about who makes things. I'm assuming that if God can send thoughts then all of God's thoughts are good, loving thoughts. If that is true, then I have to assume that there must be something capable of sending evil thoughts. It's either that or men corrupt God's thoughts. What do you think?

I am not sure I know what you mean by that word, evil. What is evil?

Evil is, well evil. It is something that is very bad!

This I do not understand. Bad, evil, where did you come up with these words?

These words are everywhere. Everyone uses them!

Many executives backdated stock options and a million people bought homes they could not afford. Does this then become your measure for validity, the number of people who believe or do something?

I see your point. I must reconsider my entire premise on the subject.

No, not at all. Do not be so easily disheartened. I sense you are onto an important thought. Carry on.

I am rather excited about it. Good and…what shall I call the opposite of good?

I don't know, what do you think is the opposite of good?

Not-good?

Excellent, good and not-good it is then.

As I said, if God can transmit good thoughts, then someone can also transmit evil thoughts.

I will forgive the habit of using that word, but try not to think in this way.

I'm sorry, I meant to say not–good thoughts, but why does it matter anyway?

We just finished talking about how your beliefs create programs that defines your reality and alters your behavior. If you continue to say "bad" or "evil" then you will create a program that not only sees the world this way, but also manifests behavior to align with your belief.

I see, and that will create a program to sustain it.

Exactly. Allow me to provoke a deeper thought and create a shift in your thinking process on this entire subject. Are you ready?

Ready? I've been ready. I have only been babbling on because you are not helping me.

What if there is no such thing that is not-good?

What! Run that by me again.

Is money animated, meaning is it alive? Does it have thoughts and a brain?

Of course it's not alive.

How can money, the physical paper itself, be good or not-good?

I think I see your point. It can't, so what then do people mean by money being good or not-good? How does this question even arise?

Money is energy, meaning it is a unit of exchange, nothing more, nothing less. Maybe it would help if you think of money in different terms. Go back in time, to before the Tang Dynasty, when copper shortages led the Chinese to issue paper notes. Go further still, to before 1500 BC when the Phoenicians invented metal money. Before these times, exchange items were animals and crops. These animals and crops were limited by the amount a family could produce on their farm. These animals and crops were neither good nor not-good. What mattered then and still does today is not the nature of the animal, but how people got animals, why they wanted the animal, and what they did with the animal after they got it.

Therefore on the question of good or not–good, the animal has nothing to do with my evaluation, only the how and why people collected animals?

Yes. Many people acquired animals to eat, breed, or work on the farm. These are all good reasons to want an animal, the "why" they sought animals. Now back in those days the way they got the animals was usually by exchanging something of like value, such as other foods, seeds, or perhaps baskets and jewelry.

You make it all sound good, but I am sure there were some people who got the animals by stealing them, for ba—not-good reasons.

Yes, that did happen. Again, however, it was not the animal that was good or not-good. None of the objects you mentioned earlier— Republicans, Democrats, sex, or money—are good or not-good. How could money possibly be not-good when it is a necessity as a unit for your bartering? The intentions behind what people do and why they do it however, can most certainly be not-good. That is a human behavior, which is quite different. If you want to identify what is not-good, you cannot judge a theology or ideology, you must evaluate the individual.

This is fascinating. The object itself, money, is neither good nor not-good. The manufacturing of paper money, or digital money is also neither good nor not-good. The evaluation of the virtue of an activity is the "how" and "why," which really boils down to the intention of the individual.

Are we finished?

Finished?

Are we finished on the topic of good and not-good?

No, we're not. I now understand what you meant when you suggested that there was no such thing as not-good...

I didn't say there was no such thing "as" not-good. I said there was no such thing that "is" not-good. There are only not-good "intentions and behaviors". You must be clear on this.

Oh my, I see your distinction now! The object "is" always good, but the behavior and intention may not be. Thank you for clarifying this. Still, that doesn't answer my question about how a good idea from God can become a not-good thing.

Give me an example of an idea that you feel is not-good and let us debate it.

Nuclear bombs.

What about them?

Good or not-good?

Use what you know.

I cannot remain detached on this. I was a nuclear submarine officer and I saw those missiles, I operated the power plants. As far as I am concerned, they were most definitely not-good.

What are we talking about?

The bombs, the missiles of course! If this idea came from God and was manifested by the hands of man, exactly how was that good?

Didn't the essence of a nuclear weapon arise from man's understanding of nuclear forces, the binding energy that holds atoms together?

Yes, that is the essence of a nuclear bomb, the release of energy when the atoms are split.

Is nuclear force a good or not-good thing?

It is neither really, just simply the nature of reality.

Might God have shared the idea of nuclear forces to help mankind understand the nature of reality?

He most certainly may have, and before you ask I will say this is definitely a good thing.

Yet, as we previously agreed, God has no hands so He most certainly did not make the weapons.

Are you telling me that once the idea was in the minds of men, it was man's idea to turn this knowledge into weapons?

I may be your friend, but you do try my patience when you insist upon forgetting everything we have already discussed and agreed upon. Who did we say swung the hammer?

Man.

Why did man do this?

It was a deterrent, to ensure peace: If every major power has nuclear weapons, then we can frighten each other into keeping peace.

Is that good or not-good? Examine the intention.

I just said it, to ensure mutual annihilation! That is not-good.

I thought you said to ensure peace. Nevertheless, have you annihilated each other yet?

No, not yet.

It appears to be a relative question, does it not?

What is it relative to?

It is relative to a point in time and where one is standing. What did humanity gain of value from understanding the nuclear forces?

We are able to send satellites into orbit and ships to the moon. That was good. I do believe there are quite a number of medical technologies and devices that were created that are also extremely useful.

Those all sound very good, are they not?

Are you saying that God gave us a good idea and man messed it up?

I didn't say anything was messed up. I said before that there was no such thing that is not-good. All ideas are good, all political parties are good, money is good, the objects are all good, but what man does with this knowledge and his intentions for doing it may be not-good. It is all relative to time and perspective.

That's what I realized when I broke my neck in January 2000. I thought it was not-good and I blamed everyone else for my physical pain and emotional suffering. Then I realized that I lived to work instead of worked to live.

What did this?

Did what?

Caused the change in perspective?

Time.

There seems to be a recurring theme here. Do you see it?

The journey may have been long, but I do believe that time provided a different vantage point for the determination of good or not-good.

Is it possible that there really is no such thing that is not-good, even an injury?

Conceptually, I can understand that everything is good over time. What I might first consider a not-good event can later serve a good purpose.

Is that all you have learned from this discussion?

No, I learned—or perhaps I should say I confirmed—that all the ideas from God are good, but what a person does with that idea and why they do it can be not-good.

~~~

WHAT IS A BELIEF?

What is a belief?

Why do you ask?

I need to know if I am making any progress? After all, it is nearly the end of the third day and I feel as if I have gone back two steps for every one I took forward.

What do you mean by two steps back and one forward?

I mean that for every question I answered, two new ones popped up.

Oh, I see. Well…I wouldn't say you went back two steps for every one forward.

Why? How do you think I'm doing?

I think you have gone back closer to three steps for every step forward.

How can you say that? I don't believe you!

Since you pride yourself on your analytical abilities, I suggest you do the math and determine your progress by yourself.

I will! Let me see, I must admit that I took a step back on thoughts, what makes things, intentions, and…uh, pain—okay fine—I think I took a step back on suffering, confusion, programs and the last discussion on goodness. However, I am absolutely certain I took a giant leap forward in deciphering my thoughts and intentions and I think I recovered from my slip with suffering. Give me a moment. Okay, that's eight steps back and three forward.

You're still suffering, but I will count that as a half, which means that if my math is correct, it is closer to my estimation.

...

Hello, are you there?

I see this trap and I refuse to answer.

What trap?

If I say I want your opinion then you will chastise me for failing to like it.

Are you saying what I believe doesn't matter, only what you believe?

...

Are you still here?

I would like a bye.

A bye, what is a bye?

It is a sporting term. But in this conversation, it is more like pleading the Fifth Amendment in the U.S. Constitution. I am legally protected from incriminating myself. By this I mean I want to skip this round of questions and move to the next level, thereby avoiding the part where I impale myself upon my own sword by virtue of the fact that I am here, asking your advice, but discarding those answers I dislike.

Your desire to skip the answers that cause you discomfort is called denial. As it is germane to the entire discussion on belief systems and how they are formed, why should I give you a bye? Do you prefer to live in ignorance?

No, no, I don't like ignorance, but don't you see it's futile? I've lost the battle on beliefs in the foreplay before I even set foot on the real fencing strip!

Now, now, you must stop beating yourself up like that just because you didn't believe you were taking so many steps back. Besides, who said life has to be a battle where there is a winner and a loser?

I hadn't thought about that, no winner or loser, what an excellent idea.

Fear not, but the road to personal freedom and salvation is filled with many setbacks. It is part of the way. As you said, we are just warming up to the topic at hand. Besides, weren't there many fencing bouts in your illustrious career, which required you to retreat to the end of your strip before you lunged forward toward ultimate victory?

Yes, of course, there were many times I had my rear foot on the edge to the strip. If I retreated another inch, I would have lost.

Than consider yourself at the edge of the fencing strip of beliefs. There is one inch between you and the abyss of ignorance. You are fighting for the gold medal of enlightenment in the universal championships. Your very presence in this battle is proof enough that you are worthy.

I don't feel worthy, and I do not believe in my own thoughts and internal guidance, which is why I am sharing my thoughts with you. Yet if I dare to admit my lack of confidence, I only further erode my limited self-esteem.

How could sharing your authentic and unique truth possibly reduce self-esteem, even if that truth is a weakness?

I need to think about this.

We have all the time that you need.

I believe you're right. If I share my truth I think it makes me stronger!

I am getting confused: Is that what you think or believe? At this moment you say you think being authentic is good, but your earlier actions demonstrated that you didn't believe that to be true. In order for this thought to be a true belief and not a momentary wish, your actions must be consistent with the words. It is only when words are transformed into actions that we can determine a legitimate belief. Which is it? Does being true to one's beliefs and convictions in the form of thoughts and actions strengthen or weaken one's constitution?

Damn! I am confused. That means I must have a program running.

Exactly! Congratulations, you just took three steps forward because you are using what you have learned!

Thank you for those kind words.

Your thanks is appreciated but unnecessary since I am merely pointing out the obvious. Now, you must find the program that is reducing your self-esteem because it needs to be evaluated and possibly deleted.

I guess I need to know if this program is outdated or faulty.

As that is true I award you another step, but only if you can name this program.

Name it? By name it do you mean label the program that makes me doubt my own unique capabilities? The program that made me grateful that you thanked me because I needed you to tell me I was moving forward. Is this the program I must name?

Yes. Now name it!

Confidence. I think it is called confidence.

You are correct. Confidence is the power generated from believing in yourself or objects greater than yourself. Confidence produces internal energy to accomplish your goals, and without it you have no beliefs and will also accomplish very little. Now, why does it matter if it is outdated or faulty?

If my confidence program is outdated, then there was a time when I was confident but now I am not, which means I doubt a legitimate belief. If it is faulty, then I believed in something that wasn't true and perhaps that false belief is being exposed.

All beliefs require confidence, and since we are talking about belief systems themselves, was there ever a time when you were chastised for debating belief systems?

A time? Are you kidding me? How about *all* the time? People don't honestly want to know your true beliefs when it comes to thorny issues, like a man loving a man, global warming, or federal spending. People don't like me when I ask questions about God, death, and past lives. Why there are hundreds of people who I thought were my friends but they have either slapped me in the face for standing up for my beliefs or they simply left my life.

Does their doubt make your belief faulty?

The answer is no. But only if I am authentic and stick to what I believe in my heart and know to be true in my soul. Being authentic is the only way to achieve progress and I cannot allow another's doubt to shatter my own beliefs. Anything else is fraudulent. But—and it's a big but—their doubts in my beliefs cause me to lose confidence.

What I believe you are telling me is that you have a program running that says if you share what you believe to be true, it rocks the world of others. Furthermore, when that happens, someone who doesn't like your belief makes you pay a price for speaking against conventional wisdom.

I think that is an excellent summary, but I'm not sure how this is helping me answer my initial question, what is a belief.

We are talking about an example of a belief, which happens to be the belief system itself. If you are certain that a belief is accurate, reliable, and true based on your personal knowledge, why would you let people rattle your confidence?

Suppose it was a friend and they were offended.

Sharing your beliefs never offends a true friend. A true friend embraces, nurtures, and helps you expand your authenticity, not diminish it. If someone you consider a friend is reducing your self-esteem, they have just revealed what side of the strip they stand on.

Hold on a minute, some true friends challenge me to help me grow.

Absolutely, but there is a huge difference in their intention. And that is the key.

Do you mean their motivations?

I said intention, which is their purpose or objective. Motivations are their reasons for their actions. My intention may be to help you, and my motivation might be fear. Do you see the difference?

I do! A friend may love me and their intention is to help, but if they are helping me out of fear, they might try to help me in an aggressive manner, whereas one who helps me out of love would be kinder.

Exactly, just like a loving parent who is motivated from their heart to teach their child for the benefit of the child. Whereas a parent who is motivated from fear may be teaching the same thing as the loving parent, but doing it so their child will get a job and move out of the house. Both had the intention to teach, but their motivations were dramatically different. Do not confuse intentions with motivations. You must understand both. Now, take the opposite kind of friend. What about a false friend, why do they challenge you?

It depends on the situation but I suspect they must be afraid they are losing control, power or feel threatened in some way. This makes them challenge the belief or do anything to stop me. But why? What is it these people believe that makes them so fearful?

You already said it. What is the belief behind tearing down your beliefs?

Oh my goodness! I see it! They believe that the world isn't big enough for the two of us to stand together and share our beliefs. They think it's a battle and a competition, and they want to be the winner and controller. If this person accepts my belief, they feel they have lost.

You said they believe life is a competition. What do you mean by competition?

Everything! Life, living, my house is better than yours. They have a belief—oh wait; this thought—it keeps expanding before I can say it.

Let it flow. What is their root belief? You're getting very close to it.

I can't quite put my finger on it but I feel like every belief system is rooted in one of two major worldviews. One group of people tears down the beliefs of others and they believe in—I'm searching for the right word—a *limited* world? And another group who believe in everyone—no not everyone, that's not right, *everything*?

The people who challenge to tear you down believe in a world of scarcity, competition, and survival of the fittest. This limited world belief is so strong and fundamental that is hardwired into their cells. They believe in separation and only see the form. They do not know the light. A program called "you-versus-me" defines all of their actions and thoughts. The other group understands that this separation is an illusion, that we are all a part of each other and everything.

I don't understand. How did this belief in separation emerge?

A belief is a collection of ideas, thoughts, and theologies that are based on experiences. Some are personal, meaning it happened to them. When they stuck their finger in a burning candle, they were burnt. Most beliefs, however, were learned from the experiences of others, at home, in school or from books.

So you are telling me they learned this from someone else? For example, I didn't experience the Civil War, but I believe it occurred.

Exactly, but how much of this experience is true?

I presume all of it, why do you ask?

Who started World War II?

The Germans started the Second World War, of course.

Really? What if you lived in China or Japan? Is that what their history books say?

I'm not Chinese or Japanese, so I wouldn't know.

It appears that the contemporary understanding of history, and by implication, beliefs, is based upon the last person who wrote the book, what side he or she belonged, and how much of the story the author told. Why else might you believe something?

My mother or father told me it was true.

Do you mean like Santa Claus or the tooth fairy?

Ha! Yes, like Santa Claus.

What if your mother and father grew up before civil liberties were popularized, when African Americans and women couldn't vote?

All these factors certainly impact a belief system, which is passed down from one generation to the next.

In this moment, do you believe China is your enemy or friend?

That's an excellent question to evaluate a belief system. I know that China is the number one or two trading partner with America and those trade agreements have lowered the cost of living for Americans by tens of thousands of dollars. A washer and dryer would cost seven times the price of the ones made in China if they were manufactured in America.

Are you telling me China is not evil? Doesn't China take advantage of child labor and pollute the environment?

Like in the United States at the turn of the century?

Are you saying that beliefs are relative to a point in time?

Yes, however not only a point in time, but the source of the original belief as well; the author, his or her location, and initial program load from parents and teachers. I think that I am starting to see how limited beliefs are formed. Travel could very well be the deathblow to ignorance.

What is the source of most people's present beliefs about international relations, global warming, national deficits, or financial investments?

I suppose that depends on many variables, such as their age, where they live, family income, and education. However, I suspect the vast majority of people today receive their information from mobile devices, the Internet, television, radio, churches, and political parties.

Is that good or not-good?

The source of the information is neither but the information the sender shares, their intentions for sharing it, and their motivations could be either.

Are these people who are sending you information trying to help you from a worldview of unity or do they believe in separation and are trying to gain control over you?

It is far bigger than me! We're talking about the world here! All the people who control the communication mediums are by definition controlling the beliefs of the world's entire population.

What about the human populations basic values and cravings? Are they controlling those as well?

Yes, all of the above.

Every one of your beliefs may have been true at one point in history, or in your parents' minds, or the teacher's classroom, or contemporary culture, but chances are that today most of them are out of date.

Why would they be out of date?

Time. Everything evolves over time.

I see your point. Everything based on physics from twenty years ago; or the history book from a hundred years ago; or even radio programs from five years ago are outdated.

Do you think it is important that your belief system is up to date?

I certainly do!

Let's recap what we have discussed. What did we say was the source of your suffering?

How can I forget! We said it was my confusion.

What caused that confusion?

It was either faulty or outdated programs that were installed in my brain.

And the essence of a program is based on what?

A belief. Every program is based on a fundamental belief and that belief commands my human control system like a robot.

How can you tell if what a person says is a true belief or just propaganda trying to control you?

If it is a true core belief, then their words are consistent with their actions.

What happens when someone tries to change your core beliefs?

It shatters my confidence and creates confusion…wait! That only happens if I allow it.

What happens if you have a core belief and you discover it is faulty. Meaning you discover it was wrong, or inaccurate.

I go into denial and try to avoid the people or situation that disclose the faulty belief.

Is this a problem? Why don't you just live with the faulty belief?

Live in ignorance, like the world is flat? Do you know what happens to life, living and evolution when you stick your head into the sand?

What?

It stops. No wait, after it has stopped for a long time, it dramatically shifts. We call these shifts scientific evolution or wars, invasions, and revolutions. Every great change, invention, new product, or medical treatment is the result of shattering an old belief. Over time, and with a new worldview, all old beliefs get shattered!

I agree. Did someone in the World of Form try to install a belief about retirement and money in an effort to modify your behaviors?

Yes…wait a minute…no. They didn't try, they did. Their beliefs became my new filter and their program executed, telling me to buy the branded shirt, the Rolex watch and take out a second mortgage to pay for it.

Yes, they did, just as I did by challenging how many steps you took and in which direction. As your friend I wanted you to grow and learn, but it does not matter: Friend or foe, either side of the debate, the result is still confusion.

You're right! I said I was confused. This is fascinating! Changing beliefs always results in a period of confusion. I'll bet the bigger and deeper the belief, the greater the confusion! I wonder if anyone ever wrote an equation or formula on how this thinking, suffering, and confusion process works. It is all very…well, confusing!

You make me laugh. Only you would consider turning human behavior into a math equation. On the other hand, I would like you to answer an important question. What are the biggest beliefs that society is trying to convince you to embrace today?

Do you mean: Taxes or no taxes, more spending or less spending, bigger government or smaller government, debt and greed are good, gays are good or evil…how much time do you have because it's a long list?

There is one belief that is the root to all these differing beliefs. We said it before, do you remember?

Are you talking about the people who are stuck in the World of Form or the doubters who don't know the light?

The doubters? The people who have an outdated worldview where you win, I lose: Take what you can get before it runs out; man is here to master an industry, make billions of dollars, and become a figure on a statue as they conquer the world. Are these the ones you are referring to?

Yes, but you left out a few things. They tried to convince me to buy what I wanted, forget about what I needed, and if I couldn't afford it, borrow the money. Those are the people I meant.

No. This is not the root belief. The doubters are just an instrument of this belief and a symptom that it exists.

There is another very important belief we have to consider if we hope to find the root belief.

What might that be?

God! What about those that say God doesn't exist, miracles cannot be explained, prayers are wishful thinking, and angels are a figment of my imagination?

True, these people have a limited worldview, but what is the core limiting belief?

I've got it! They don't believe they have a soul.

No, they might believe they have a soul. What they don't believe is that they "are" a soul.

~~~

Day Four—

COINCIDENCE, INITIATIONS AND CONFIRMATIONS

WHAT IS A COINCIDENCE?

What is a coincidence?

A what?

A coincidence.

I don't know where you come up with these words but you certainly have a great many. Give me an example so I can help you answer the question.

Remember when I first injured my neck on the submarine in 1985?

I do.

One day, while listening to my music on shuffle mode, I was writing my personal journal about this incident. As I wrote, "I struck a beam with the center of my forehead. As my

73

neck snapped back, my hardhat flew off...I fell to the ground unconscious," a song by Sugarland was playing. The name of the song is "It Happens." One second after I finished typing that line the singer sang, "Sorry about your neck honey."

Does this happen often?

Sometimes twice a day, at least for me. I don't know about everyone else. Another time I wrote a journal entry about the time I was supervising the Valdez oil spill clean up, and as a joke after an unfortunate incident, I typed, "Go to jail...do not pass go...do not collect $200."

Why would you go to jail? Did they try to put you in jail for this oil spill?

It's a reference to a game called Monopoly. It was a joke.

Is it funny? I don't see the humor.

Have you ever played Monopoly?

No.

You should try it sometime.

Perhaps one day. Carry on with your story.

As soon as I typed that comment about going to jail, a man on the television show that my sister was watching asked, "Do you need a get-out-of-jail card?"

Did you say yes?

You're missing the point. I didn't need a card.

You are confusing me; I thought you needed to get out of jail. Wouldn't that card help you?

The point is that this was another coincidence.

Oh, I see now. I told you I didn't understand that word.

These two stories are examples of what we call a coincidence!

Now I understand.

What are they? How did this happen?

How did what happen?

How is it that two independent events, my written words and the song playing, can accidentally share the same message at the exact same time?

Accidentally? Why would you say that? There was no accident.

I mean it happened by chance.

By chance do you mean luck?

Luck means that the probability of these events happening at the same time is very low, so yes. In fact, I calculated the chance of those words coming out at any random time from over 1,000 songs playing. The possibility of her saying "Sorry about your neck, honey" is about once every fifty hours. Why did that happen the second I wrote those words?

I just don't understand how you become so confused. I am beginning to believe it is all the words you use that make no sense. There is no such thing as chance, or luck, and it certainly wasn't an accident.

What do you call a coincidence?

I understand you think of them as accidents, but to me they are synchronicities and there is no luck involved.

Why is that?

You made them happen. Subconsciously, of course.

How could I make them happen?

It was your intentions. You created a thought and you sent it out into the universe, and God responded. Really, it is all I can do to keep from laughing…chance, accidents. Do you retain anything we talk about?

Okay, I'll call it a synchronicity. Why then does it happen sometimes and not all the time?

It is related to the laws of synchronicity.

There are laws about this? Is there a police force too?

In a universe where nothing is an accident, there are laws for everything. The problem is that most people fail to see or understand them because they live in the World of Form, and the understanding of the light is now dark. They rely on science to explain these phenomena, but since science does not understand the World of Light it cannot explain them.

Please explain these laws so that I might understand synchronicities.

I am not going to repeat what we already discussed about intentions and how you make events happen.

Energy? It's energy isn't it?

Nor will I repeat what we learned about thoughts and how they transcend time and space, or how they are sent and received by your brain.

I remember they are all shared and interconnected, and we are all simultaneously sending and receiving thoughts, and that they travel at the speed of light.

Do you remember what we discussed about beliefs and programs just yesterday?

I have not forgotten! You must think my mind is a sieve.

No, I think your mind is at times not thinking. When an experience falls outside of your belief system you go into denial, pretending it didn't happen. The mind is unable to piece together the true reality because of deeply rooted and limited programs that are fighting to survive. If you discover even one of them, your subconscious mind knows that you will uninstall it. You become confused and the false belief expands. The mind refuses to accept the inconsistency, and then it creates words—like accident or coincidence—to explain the contradictions.

I believe I am starting to understand the picture. If I have this correct, the implications are that everything in the World of Form is a façade, an illusion.

Go back to your synchronicity now. A minute ago, you asked why they didn't happen all the time. In fact they do, when the proper laws are established and fulfilled.

Now will you explain the laws?

Think of them as conditions. There are four: Good intentions, focus, presence, and a need.

What do you mean by presence?

You are awake, present, in the moment, all that power-of-now stuff. You do understand the power of being in the now, don't you?

Yes, yes, I read some of those books. I understand being present and in the moment, not living in the past or worrying about the future. I just wasn't sure what you meant by presence.

Do you understand what you needed?

Clearly, I didn't and still don't. What did I need when these synchronicities occurred?

You needed help. A synchronicity is nothing more than a confirmation.

You're telling me that a synchronicity happens when I am living in the moment, with good intentions and require assistance? Is that it?

Yes. You were being assisted, helped by God, guides, and guardian angels. I think you call them the crowd upstairs or some nonsense like that, as if there is a stairway that leads you off the earth's surface.

What were they confirming? I mean, why did these coinci…I mean synchronicities occur on those two occasions?

Isn't it obvious?

No, it is not obvious. It hasn't quite sunk in yet.

The reason isn't clear to you because you have a collection of words that are inaccurate and distort the true nature of reality. In your quest for truth you discovered that the incidents with your neck were a wake-up call, intending to help you discover your true identity and purpose for this life. If you change your words and discard the faulty beliefs from the World of Form, you will realize that God was confirming that with his messages.

Why was it necessary?

We already said that you were living in a world of illusions, trapped in your mind, beliefs, and programs. Once you completely believe that you "are" a soul from the World of Light, you will see how you are being guided and protected every single moment.

That makes a lot of sense.

Why?

While I was bedridden I was very depressed. One day I said a prayer in silence, *why did you do this to me?* Within five minutes my three-year-old son, Grant, wiggled the handle and opened the door, pranced in, and said, "Daddy, you work too hard."

You see, God confirmed it for you.

Yes, but I didn't know this at the time. The next day I said another prayer in silence, "God, what do you want me to do?" Again, within a few minutes, Grant opened the door, and this time he bounced in on his toes and said, "Daddy, you need to play!"

Uh huh, I get the feeling this isn't over. Go on.

I couldn't believe this was happening! I then calculated the probability and it was one in a million of him doing this two times in a row.

Science has really polluted your mind, you know. Please don't tell me you did it again.

I did! However, this time it was a test! I asked, "God, how are you doing this?" Grant once again appeared from no where and this time he said, "Remember, remember!"

Oh my!

What?

This wasn't just a synchronicity.

What do you mean, not "just" a synchronicity?

It was an initiation.

What's an initiation?

We will get into that in a minute. First, you must finish your story. What happened next?

I calculated the probability again, and it was one in a billion that this was luck or chance. I just couldn't believe it!

Of course you couldn't, which is why we are having this dialogue in the first place.

What do you mean, why are we talking?

The initiation! You fail to believe! You lacked trust then and after all these years of reading, researching, testing, calculating probabilities you still do not trust in God. You may believe that God is real, but you are not ready to put your life in his hands with complete trust.

I believe you; at least, I do now.

Really? There is a pattern emerging here. Do you see it?

I think there is more than one pattern.

I see two.

Is one about beliefs?

Yes, and the pattern is that you say you believe with your words but you fail to demonstrate that you believe in your actions. You must align your thoughts and your body to move in the same direction, otherwise this discrepancy will continue to rip you in half.

Is the other pattern about time?

No.

What is the other pattern?

What you called a coincidence is really a synchronicity, a confirmation from the divine that is pointing you to your life path, the reason your soul incarnated in this body. God does not intervene without a good reason. These were big interventions, which is why I said it was an initiation.

What is the second pattern?

You keep thinking and studying the signs and science behind it all, hoping to rationalize the phenomenon so you can deny why you are here. You are doing everything you can to refuse your calling and the divine is saying, "Okay, have it your way."

WHAT IS INITIATION?

Are you telling me that if I don't take God's advice or follow His signs then God is going to allow me to just keep suffering?

Do your teenage children ever throw their dirty clothes on the floor?

All the time, why?

Do you go in their room and pick up after them and do their wash?

No, my wife taught them to do their own laundry.

What happens if they don't pick up their clothes or do their laundry?

Then their room is a mess, they can't find anything, and they don't have any clean clothes to wear to school.

What do they eventually learn from this?

After a week of people avoiding them in school they grow up and do their own laundry.

And you think that God is any different then a sensible parent? He's saying you have some dirty clothes in your spiritual closet and now you are old enough to clean it out. That is what I meant by a spiritual initiation.

You said that before and I didn't really understand the difference between an intervention and an initiation.

An intervention is when someone or something steps in to stop you or help you. An initiation is completely different.

What's an initiation?

How old is Grant now?

He's fifteen. Is this relevant?

Yes, pay attention. Since you broke your neck twelve years ago, have you and your son bonded in any special ways?

When he was five, I taught him how to use tools and make his first pinewood derby car. It was pretty funny: The design he chose was shaped like a dog bone, thin in the middle with a wide front and rear. When he finished carving up the wooden block it was so mauled and disfigured that it looked like a chewed-up dog bone. That night, I took a small amount of wood putty and began to reshape it. I did this every night for the next week until the shape was restored. Of course, he never knew and thought that he had carved a perfectly shaped car.

How did he do in the race?

He took first place that year, and for the next four years as well!

That's wonderful. What did you teach him from all this?

I taught him how to use a saw, work with wood tools, and practice safe habits like wearing safety goggles. With practice he also got better at the whole carving process.

Did you teach him other things, like how to shave?

Indeed I did. It was hard to find anything that needed shaving, but he was adamant that he needed to learn.

What about shooting a gun, fishing, hunting, did you teach him any of these things?

Yes, of course, we are Texans you know. I taught him to shoot rifles and pistols, how to use a bow and arrow, and I even taught him to fence. We even grew fond of playing Stratego together, but that didn't work out so well.

Why is that?

He beats me. Bad.

Well, you win some and lose some with sons. Now, when a father teaches a son these various lessons, what does your generation call these events?

They are rites of passage, rituals, or ceremonies that mark the end of one cycle and the beginning of another.

You were teaching your son how to grow up and become a man?

Yes.

The event when you broke your neck was a rite of passage as well, but not for you as a man. It was for your soul. What I find most interesting is the role your son played. Apparently, the two of you have a strong soul bond.

I thought you said it was an initiation.

No, I said that what you and your son had was a soul bond. Apparently the two of you have an agreement in this life and he is here to assist you.

Man, there is a lot going on here. I'm not sure I know what all this means.

Yes you do. You just have to piece it together. Try.

We just discussed that God answering my silent prayers was not an accident, rather a confirmation. God was confirming that my injury was a wake-up call to set me on the right path for this lifetime.

What did the experience of breaking your neck, your wake-up call help you to learn?

I worked too hard and I needed to play.

What did that mean to you?

I was living to work instead of working to live. I wasn't happy. I was not following my heart.

What did you learn? You've told me before, but now I want you to skip the details and look at it from a higher level, from your soul's point of view.

I learned that I was suffering and why I was suffering. Then I learned why I wasn't happy and…then I quit my high-paying job and created television shows, games, and a radio show.

What were you doing with all these shows and games?

I was creating, having fun, and…exploring…no, not exploring. I was searching…that's it! I was on a quest!

What was the purpose of the quest?

At first I wanted to know how God could answer a silent prayer through my son, but the more I read and searched the more confused I became.

Tell me what confused you.

I grew up a man of science, a math major, completely structured and logical. But I desperately wanted to know how these phenomena could happen. How does a synchronicity work, how can a person send and receive thoughts? Is it divine? Can God do it? How does He do it? The list of questions just grew and grew and grew.

Would it be safe to say that this all began with you breaking your neck?

What a ridiculous question. Of course!

This began your quest you say. Can you give me another name for a quest?

It is a pursuit or a mission. Mine became an obsession.

Obsession. Why do you use that word?

I spent ten years and a lot of money traveling the world, reading every book I could find, interviewing hundreds of people, and probing thousands of research papers.

What happened to your material World of Form?

It fell apart. I didn't care about that world. I *had* to know; I had to find the answers to the questions that were driving me crazy.

Tell me what exactly happened to make you not care about the World of Form?

I started to see the faulty and outdated programs. I saw a world full of people who cared only about money, but not how they acquired it. Then I saw them buying things they didn't need, only to fill an empty hole inside like I had. I noticed that our planet was being destroyed; trust and integrity abused. Then I tried to be more loving and caring, and people took advantage of my trust and love. That really confused me, so I retreated to a cave of sorts, shielding myself from a world that filled me with more suffering and confusion.

Let's review. You broke your neck a second time when you were a powerful CEO, which wasn't an "accident." It was a program in your subconscious mind, an unconscious intention because you secretly disliked your job—but your conscious mind was unaware. Do I have it right so far?

Sadly, yes.

Why do you say sadly?

Oops, I was thinking in terms of the World of Form, where things can be bad.

How would you rephrase it in the World of Light, as a being who knows he doesn't just have a soul, rather he is a soul?

My soul knew I wasn't happy and that I wasn't fulfilling my purpose, so it created a way to wake me up! Since my conscious mind was switched off, my soul needed to get my attention, which is why the synchronicities happened. They confirmed for me that I was on my path.

Ah yes, the path, the journey, the way. However, this wasn't any normal journey, it was special.

Why would you say that?

How many people do you know that spend ten years travelling the world, nearly bankrupting themselves, all in search of answers to humanity's oldest questions? How many ignore offers to be an executive and make tons of money, only to strike out on their own as entrepreneurs?

Yes, I see now. It was a bit obsessive.

I believe it was more than obsessive; it was a desperate and compulsive quest. Use your logical mind, and turn it into a formula. Ask yourself this: What percent of millionaires spend almost all of their net worth on a philosophical quest?

I see your point, and I am humbled and grateful for you helping me see this from a broader view.

I said it before. This was not just your run-of-the-mill, good-morning alarm, where God says, "Wake up, restore your health, spend more time with your family." It was a spiritual initiation, which is a series of tests and trials that your soul has to experience to achieve self-realization.

Why did I have to experience all these things?

So you could fulfill your purpose.

Now I am beginning to understand. My soul took control of my fire-control system, launched a nuclear missile at my mind and ego, and then took the keys to the car and went on a road trip to discover what I needed to know.

What was the initiation about?

It was the end of my mental and physical development and the beginning of my spiritual quest to find my purpose and learn lessons.

AUM.

What's that?

Purpose—akara, ukara, and makara—you know it as amen.

What language is that?

Sanskrit.

Are you going to explain why you said AUM, or keep me in suspense?

I'll explain it when we get to your question on purpose.

How did you know I have a question on my purpose?

Must be a coincidence.

—◠◠◠—

WHAT ARE TRUTH BUMPS?

Oh, my Lord! I can't believe what just happened.

What?

I got goose bumps.

Here we go again. What is a goose bump?

It's a truth bump, a confirmation! It means that what you said, about the initiation and my purpose, is true! There are no accidents!

I know what a confirmation is but I have never heard of a truth bump or goose bump.

When you get goose bumps all the hair on your body stands up, as if your hair were a metal fiber and you passed a magnet over it. They are a pretty common experience for me. I was actually just thinking about them.

You mean you had a synchronicity?

C'mon, I know that this isn't news to you, but it is for me. When you spoke of synchronicities I was wondering if a goose bump was also a form of confirmation and as soon as I had the thought, boom! Goose bumps!

That was definitely a synchronicity. It's another form of confirmation, nothing more. You are correct.

I accept that, but what I want to know is, how exactly does this work?

Tell me what you know about your body. I mean at a cellular level.

My body is pure energy, and my brain is sending and receiving information from every cell in my body. There are a hundred trillion cells in my body. That means every billionth of a second my brain is sending hundreds of trillions of electrical impulses to cells. Each cell knows everything about every system in my body. To put it into perspective, each cell has more knowledge and information than the Library of Congress.

Yes, yes, that's all very interesting, but what does this all mean?

I have a theory.

What's your theory?

I believe I am surrounded by guardians and angels, and when I am about to say something that is a deep truth, I think they get excited. Their excitement causes all my cells to electrify, making my hair stand up on end.

Interesting theory, but of course it can never be proven. Perhaps it is nothing more than your nervous system twitching.

That can't be.

Why?

It must have to do with energy particles outside my body.

Why would you say that?

It happened when you said it, not me! I can be talking to someone on the phone and before they say something, my body will light up in truth bumps.

How could you prove this theory?

I suppose you could measure my brainwaves and put sensors on my body. Then, have people share thoughts with me, some of which are true and others of which are false and measure the results.

Yes, you could, but isn't this happening all the time?

Isn't what happening all the time?

People saying things that are true and you don't get truth bumps.

You might be onto something here. There is at least one other condition that must be necessary, something I'm missing.

Something you're missing?

Yes, you know, something I am not thinking of.

I see. By this do you mean something that is not conscious?

Exactly. Something unconscious.

. . .

Hello?

Yes.

Why aren't you saying anything?

I don't know.

How can you not know?

. . .

Well?

You don't honestly expect me to know what I don't know, do you?

. . .

Now you are the one that is silent.

. . .

Perhaps why you don't know what you don't know is the same reason you have a truth bump and do not know why.

I'd accuse you of having a secret, but there are no secrets between us.

I have shared nothing with you that you didn't already know. You simply have to remember.

I fail to understand why you always talk in riddles, but I have simply come to accept it.

You fail to understand, you imply I have secrets, and you have truth bumps for reasons you cannot remember. Is any of this sounding familiar?

It must be a program running on stealth mode again. Something…oh my! I just got the chills.

The chills.

That's another term for truth bumps—uh…I mean goose bumps. Whatever!

I figured that one out all on my own.

I got the truth bumps when I said it was a program running on stealth mode. That's the missing condition. The truth has to be something that I either refused to accept, or failed to see.

I believe you are close but there is one more element. Think about our last conversation about initiation, purpose, and intention.

Every time they are present, something is pointing me on my spiritual path, another soul-purpose confirmation. Is that it?

None of the confirmations, including truth bumps, are meaningless occurrences. All these synchronicities, God answering prayers through your son, signs, and wonders, they are special forms of communications. They are all guiding you to your higher purpose.

DAY FIVE —

DEATH, SOULS AND MATTER

WHAT IS NEAR-DEATH?

All this talk of synchronicities, confirmations, and initiations reminds me of an unusual set of circumstances that happened to me.

Unusual, yes, these experiences are most unusual. Assuming of course you live in the World of Form and are unaware of the subtle workings of the universe and World of Light.

I'm beginning to understand.

Tell me what happened.

It was back when I attended the United States Naval Academy. I was sailing my boat hard into the wind for a practice race. I had on three layers of clothing—it was freezing. My hands were cramping from the cold and from gripping the mainsheet, so I alternated holding it between my hands and teeth.

Why do I get the feeling that this was not a good idea?

I checked the time on the new wristwatch my father had given me on my eighteenth birthday. It was the only gift I'd ever received directly from him, and the last thing he gave me before he died three months later from malignant melanoma.

My teeth ached from holding the mainsheet, so I switched to holding it with my left hand. After I wrapped the sheet twice around my wrist I let go with my mouth. But my arms were weak, and the force from the sail yanked my hand into the pulley.

Did that hurt?

No. The watch protected my wrist from the pulley, but the watchband snapped open from the pressure. My precious gift went flying across the deck and straight into the river. I dropped everything and dove into the water after it.

Was that a wise thing to do? The water was cold and you were wearing a lot of clothing.

All I could think about was saving the watch! As I swam down I saw it seesawing back and forth like a leaf falling from a tree. I reached left, but it zigged right; I reached right, and it zagged left. I swam deeper and deeper, five feet, eight feet, and then ten feet beneath the hull of my drifting boat. I was fifteen feet beneath the surface, still going down. Everything else was meaningless.

I can see it now. This was a defining moment.

You have no idea. I could see my watch still sinking, but I had to make a choice between a precious gift from my deceased father and my life. I turned to go back up, but my clothes acted like anchors. I tried to remove them, but my extremities were not functioning properly, and my lungs were desperate for air.

I sense an intervention coming. What happened next?

Finally, my boots came off. But my foul-weather gear was fatally stubborn. I pulled off the jacket. I tore at the suspender snaps, but they refused to release their grips. My efforts were becoming futile. My lungs were bursting to expel the depleted air that was fighting hard to get out, and finally they exploded. A plume of air escaped from my mouth and nose, and I sucked in a large gulp of cold water. I started choking. My body convulsed. And then I saw a beacon, twinkling stars, and shimmering lights. How blissful. I said a silent prayer, Dear God, please save me.

You went through the gateway didn't you?

How did you know?

Because you were dying, I can see it. I see through your eyes, remember?

Yes well, you're right, but I didn't know it at the time. At least, I didn't remember. All I remembered was climbing out of the water and getting back into the boat.

When did you find out? I mean about what really happened.

This is the really bizarre part. It was twenty-seven years later, and I was living in Singapore at the time. A friend encouraged me to have a psychic read my aura. I didn't know I had one. "Will it hurt?" I asked. She laughed. "Of course not." As I sat in the chair, the psychic rubbed his hands together, closed his eyes, and told me to relax. Silence enveloped the room, and then he spoke. "When you were twenty years old you nearly drowned."

He could see it in your aura. Powerful.

Then he said, "It had something to do with your father."

As you can imagine, I was paralyzed; I fell back into the memories. No one knew. "You need to stop denying what happened," he said. Meanwhile, I was reliving the drowning, choking, and clutching at my throat. I felt the ice in my veins, the wind, and the feeling of water surging into my lungs. I stuttered, then asked, "I'm...I'm supposed to deny that I lost my...my watch?"

"That's not what I am talking about," he said tenderly.

I began to shake as drops of sweat trickled out of my palms faster than the words dripped from my mouth. "What...are... you...saying?"

"You have to stop denying how you were saved."

"I don't remember," I said. "How...was...I...saved?"

What did he say?

"Michael."

Michael, who?

That's what I asked him, Michael who? "Archangel Michael," he replied.

Michael did save you.

Yes, that's what he said.

You have been protected your entire life. You are being called. It must be important.

Well, I didn't believe it. Not for one second.

There is more though, isn't there?

Yes, indeed there is. Over the next eight years, there were no less than five total strangers who came up to me and told me that I was saved by Archangel Michael.

The man of science didn't have a formula for it.

No, I didn't.

When did you remember the tunnel and the other side?

As more and more people told me, I eventually went to one of the top psychologists in the world. He regressed me. During regression I remembered, I saw the tunnel and I remembered it all.

That's beautiful. Clearly, you are blessed.

I was so fascinated by it all that I became certified in hypnosis. I have since regressed myself many times; it is quite a moving experience.

Did you ever do past-life regressions?

Yes. In one life, apparently the happiest life of many, I was a woman with six children. I lived in a seaport village in Italy by the name of Positano. My family and I owned and operated a restaurant.

How can you be certain this wasn't your imagination?

There was a series of amazing synchronicities and confirmations that helped me to see it wasn't my imagination.

Will you share them with me?

Yes! After I viewed this life I went to visit my cousin in Sydney, Australia. She took me out to dinner, and a good friend of hers from Italy came to join us.

Keep going.

I forget his name, but I will never forget his shirt! He walks over and sits down, and I couldn't take my eyes off his shirt. It says "Positano" on it.

Ha! How funny!

That's not the best part. Just wait. Having never been there and with the past-life image fresh in my mind, I ask him, "What do you do in Positano?"

"Oh," he says, "My family has a restaurant on the ocean."

Oh my! What a wonderful confirmation!

I'm not finished yet!

There's more?

I was so energized that I called a dear friend of mine who is a total believer in these experiences. She lived in Singapore, and her name is Helena. She didn't answer, so I left a message telling her that I had the most amazing story to share. The next day I got a text message. You are *not* going to believe what it said!

I shall not even attempt a guess.

"Hi Jon, sorry to miss ur call. On vacation, eating in a fabulous restaurant overlooking the ocean…in *POSITANO!*"

…

Well?

Well what?

No reaction?

It's not as if this is all new to me you know. I was contemplating the meaning of it all.

What to you think it all meant?

When you were a child, did your father take your exams for you?

No, why do you ask?

I just keep wondering where you get the idea that I am supposed to do all your thinking for you.

...

Stop looking at me with those pleading eyes.

...

Okay, I'll summarize it for you this time, but don't expect me to do this again.

...

What we have here is a near-death experience, where an Angel saved you. Some day you must ask yourself why. Second, you have confirmation from multiple sources over many years that you were saved by Michael. Third, you experienced going through the gateway, and you have confirmations of past-life experiences. What is it going to take to convince you that death is not the end, God holding a sign in your face?

Well, it's funny you should say that.

~~~

WHAT IS A SOUL?

God actually held a sign in front of your face telling you that death is not the end. What do you mean?

In my quest to understand the nature of life, living, and reality I launched a radio program called Global Evolution. I talked about everything related to national, corporate, social, and human evolution. I always started the show by saying "To our listeners around the world, good morning, good afternoon, and good evening, as Global Evolution is listened to in over a hundred countries."

That's a nice introduction.

I thought so too, that's why I said it. I wanted listeners to recognize this was a show for the world not simply America. I interviewed the world's greatest thinkers in theology, physics, biology, philosophy, and social changes. You name it, I researched it.

What did you ask them?

I asked them everything: Who and what is God, how "can" God communicate with us, is DNA the language of God, what is a sign, or a coincidence, how can thoughts transcend time and space, and one of my favorites—does a company have a soul?

How many people did you interview?

About three hundred over four years, but that's not the point right now. The point is that one of the women I interviewed on self-help called me up after our interview and offered to do a "reading" for me.

Aha, she was a psychic!

I didn't know that at the time, I just thought she was a self-help expert. Anyway, I said sure. Well, the first thing she said was that I almost drowned when I was young, and Archangel Michael saved me. I said thank you, but I knew that already. *Then* she told me something that was both shocking and made me cry. She said, "There is someone on the other side who says he loves you."

By the other side, you mean a soul that has passed over.

Yes. I asked "Who?" She replied, "He is calling you daddy, and he says he is your son." "I don't have a son who died," was my baffled response. The psychic then told me, "He says he would be about nineteen years old, and his name is Michael."

Take your time; I can see reliving this is an emotional experience.

Well…when she said that, the floor dropped out of my world.

I thought you said you didn't have a son that died. Did you?

She was talking about something that no one knew except my wife and me.

What was it?

Marianne had a miscarriage before our first daughter was born. If it was a boy we were going to name him Michael.

…Yes, I'd agree that's a sign from God. We are pure energy and energy does not die, it is merely transformed.

WHAT IS MATTER?

What is matter?

Matter, does matter really matter?

That's exactly what I was thinking!

I'm not even going to ask.

I don't care if you sent the thought to me, or me to you.

It doesn't matter. What matters most is that we understand that thought transference is a real phenomenon.

Precisely!

Now, why the question on matter? I sense the scientist has a problem.

I do, and it's a big one. As you might very well imagine, I was deep in the rabbit hole by the time the psychic told me she knew about Michael. I'd had precognitive visions, prayed to God who answered through my son, discovered I was saved by Archangel Michael, and of course now my unborn son is telling me he loves me from the other side.

It's all quite beautiful, isn't it?

It is now, but it wasn't then.

Why? What happened next?

That's why I brought up the subject of matter! That's when I went on my ten-year quest. I started taking every class and course I could imagine. I became certified in Reiki, remote viewing, hypnosis, past life regression, meditation, and yoga. Of course, I prayed a lot as well! In fact, I started going to all different types of churches, reading the Bible, Bhagavad–Gita, the history of religion, and history of science.

What does this have to do with "matter"?

It has to do with my neck. When I broke it, the doctors fused 3 vertebrae into one solid piece of bone. I have the X-rays and MRIs to prove it. Five years after the surgery, after five years of doing everything I could think of to heal my neck and body—Chinese medicine, acupuncture, herbal teas, meditation, running energy, yoga, and massage—I went for a check up. I thought it was routine, but after an X-ray the doctor called and asked me to do an MRI. Then after the MRI he had me do a CT scan. Then he called me into his office. I was living in Singapore at the time, and my two doctors were the best in the country. They operated on most of the politicians and royalty in Asia.

Where are you going with this?

My doctors had over eighty years of experience between them. They called me into their office and they showed me the X-rays from five years ago when 3 vertebrae were one solid piece of bone. Then they showed me the latest results and… one of my vertebrae had returned. They said it was a miracle!

Did you show these to any doctors in America?

Yes, they said that clearly my neck was never fused.

Denial.

It's right there on the pictures, and I think that if I did something to break my neck after the fusion I would have known.

How did you resolve this contradiction?

I interviewed a Nobel laureate in physics and I asked him, "Does matter matter?" He told me that what we used to think of as matter when I was a kid—objects we can touch and feel—was decades out of date. Scientists discovered another kind of matter, which they call dark matter.

Dark? Do you mean evil?

Very funny, there is no such thing, remember?

I couldn't resist.

They call it dark matter because it was discovered in black holes. Moreover, dark matter is not physical, meaning you can't touch it. What he said was that we now call the other kind of matter, the kind you can touch, "ordinary matter." Now here's the fascinating part. The non-physical dark matter is about 95 percent of everything: Me, water, trees, stars, planets, universe, everything.

You say it cannot be touched?

No, it can't.

This surprises you?

It did at the time. Does it surprise you?

Why don't you take a breath, get out of your head, and open your mind to the present while I transmit thoughts your way?

All right, give me a minute.

Take a few breaths, clear your mind. Focus on your body and remember what the Nobel laureate told you. Can you remember?

I remember.

He told you that matter was not solid, that it was filled with empty space. But space is not empty; it is teeming with trillions of particles of energy.

Yes, he did.

Even the ordinary matter, the protons and electrons, are not solid, but positive and negative forces holding together the only solid matter, a tiny neutron.

Yes.

He told you that the glue holding the proton and neutron together to form atoms is a binding energy, which of course, is not solid.

Indeed he did.

You then concluded that your neck was not solid; that matter as you thought of it, was more than 95 percent not-solid. Now, what have you learned from our discussion that implies that none of these metaphysical phenomena are so hard to understand?

My brain is a supercomputer sending and receiving trillions of thoughts, which are nothing but energy particles. These thought waves, or energy particles, are a part of everything and everyone. When I healed my neck I was tuning myself to the frequency of my bones and manipulating the particles based on my intentions.

Spooky, isn't it?

I assume you are referring to quantum entanglement, what Einstein once called spooky behavior. If so, yes, there is certainly an abundance of scientific observations about the interaction of energy particles that science does not understand. Nevertheless, hundreds of experiments confirm the phenomenon. Einstein said that when we think about things, the things we think about change. He was talking about how our thoughts affected electrons. I cannot be certain what he meant, but what that means to me is quite obvious: Our thoughts affect physical reality.

Does matter matter, the kind of matter you learned about in school in the 1960s?

Only to the people whose institutions, funding, or research are attached to the World of Form.

Isn't every holy book in the world filled with stories of healing hands and miracles like you had when your vertebra returned? Experiences that even a hundred years ago science couldn't explain but now science can?

I believe so, but I cannot be certain as I have not read or studied every holy book.

Trust me, miracles are in every major holy book.

Why isn't this knowledge, the science behind prayers and energy and the power to heal from within, more widely understood? Who or what would want to stop people from understanding the essence of a miracle?

The answer to the question is in the question itself.

I see. A miracle, by definition, is a wonderful event that cannot be explained by science or natural laws. It is the domain of religions.

Now, rephrase the question.

Who or what would want to stop humanity from understanding the essence of a wonderful event that belongs to the domain of religions?

Drum roll please…the answer is?

The old worldview and definition of matter no longer applies to scientists; they already blew it up and now refer to things we can touch as "ordinary matter." So then it would have to be holy men, the ones who still cling to the outdated and faulty definition of matter.

Matter only matters to religious institutions that have no stake in accepting that miracles can be explained by science.

They can't do that!

Do what?

Religious people cannot deny the existence and logic of science!

Why is that?

It's a paradox.

How so?

We said in our discussions about what makes things that all thoughts originate from God and that the essence of all ideas and inventions were inspired from the will of God and implemented by the hands of man. To deny that scientific ideas are the will of God is to deny that all inspiration and ideas originate with God. It's a religious paradox.

True. Unless a holy man creates the concept of evil and tells people that some scientific ideas originate from a devil.

Yes, I see how that solves his contradiction...but not mine! I am reminded of something you said earlier.

What is that?

You said there are no contradictions and when I find one—like a religion not wanting to endorse how science can explain miracles—then you have to reexamine your assumptions. We said there is no thing that is not-good! That means the assumption of a devil, as currently understood by many, is impossible.

Correct, all objects are good when examined in relation to an extended period of time. A war may at first appear terrible but humanity eventually learns an important lesson. But there is a revelation unfolding here, and it is much bigger than the devil.

What is that?

The debate we are having on the subject of matter is shattering an illusion.

What illusion is that?

As you examine the assumptions and contradictions you are beginning to shatter the illusion that science is somehow different from faith. Eventually, there will come a time, and soon, when the convergence of science and faith will occur and the nature of matter and miracles will be revealed.

WHAT IS DEVIOUS?

That is the third rail. I'm not touching that!

Third rail? What do you mean by third rail?

The third rail on the train tracks is the one that carries all the power. Touch it and you'll be electrified!

Why would you be electrified?

The religious paradox, the contradictions and illusions we just talked about. I just concluded that there are at least two other assumptions I was making, and debating, and to challenge either is a CLI.

What is a CLI?

CLI is navy slang for a career-limiting incident.

Tell me about these two assumptions that create a CLI.

First of all, I have always assumed that organized religions want to promote miracles. Now I have to reconsider that assumption. I mean come on; there is no logical reason that the world should not know how to heal using hands. It's in the Bible for heavens sake!

Are there not others that don't want you to know this?

Do you mean the entire western medical and pharmaceutical industry?

That would be two more possible institutions that don't want science to explain miracles.

Yes, but that was the first assumption and not the biggest CLI.

What is the biggest assumption?

The biggest assumption is that I always assumed there was a devil. Telling people there is no devil would not go over well, which in and of itself is a contradiction. You would think everyone would shout for joy to learn there is no devil.

You are beginning to see that the World of Form is filled with contradictions and assumptions.

If the devil is a manmade construct created by people to justify which thoughts they deem good and which thoughts they deem not-good, then the foundation of some churches begin to crack. Just imagine the implications

Give me one.

Okay, if I assume that there is no evil then wars actually serve a purpose! God's purpose no less! That's a third rail!

You have a problem with this?

I think you've gone mad!

That or everyone else is mad. I wonder which it is.

I know what Einstein would say.

What?

"You can never solve a problem on the level on which it was created."

What does that mean?

It means if you want to answer the questions about God, a devil, good, and evil, you cannot think like a person who created them. You have to get outside their box.

Give me an example of getting outside the box of science, religion, or even politics.

Okay, go back to any war and think about all the people who suffered and died!

Died? What do you mean they died?

Fine. I'm outside the box, there is no such thing as death, they're a soul, and death isn't the end. Nevertheless, how could something like World War II be good?

When you pray to God asking for him to make you courageous, does he sprinkle you with pixie dust and poof! You're courageous?

No, in fact the opposite is true.

What do you mean?

He throws every fear in my face, so I can become courageous. In one respect, it is sort of devious, but on another, God is like a parent. Again, he won't do my laundry but he will teach me how.

How many wars, cases of genocide, and aboriginal atrocities have there been throughout modern times? How many "holy" wars? Ask yourself, who destroyed the Mayan and Incan knowledge? Who destroyed the Native American Indians, who destroyed all the Hindu temples and why did they do this? If you were God, what would you do?

You're asking me to explain the reasons for war and how God would think.

We'll get to war and love later, but that is not what I am asking you.

What is the question?

What would God do?

Create a war to end all wars to teach his children a lesson.

Go back to you now. What did you learn from your pain and suffering?

I discovered who I am, why I am here, and my purpose. And I found God.

Did we or did we not just agree that God doesn't have pixie dust; he can't just sprinkle you with knowledge and understanding; it is something you must learn by yourself?

As distasteful as it may seem, I must piece the puzzle together. What I perceived as pain was really optional suffering, created by my own mind. I understand why it was good; I believe in God and I believe in souls. I am a soul in a body and I have lived many lives. I believe that death is not the end but merely a transition. I believe and understand all these things but I am at a loss as to the larger picture, as seen from the eyes and ears and brain of God.

Keep going. You are on the right track and have more to learn. What is the conclusion you have yet to state? Where does this all lead you?

I don't have a conclusion.

Yes, you do. What did you learn from all those radio interviews?

I met a man who was homeless as a child and became a builder; a young girl who was a gifted artist but raped by her father, so she became a child sexual therapist using art; a lifelong atheist who became a Christian Scientist; a skeptical psychotherapist who became a past-life regression healer.

How did they find their peace?

Through their pain and suffering.

Just like you. No pixie dust.

Just like me.

Give me an example of a few who did not achieve this realization.

A District Attorney who prosecuted pornography and loved hookers; a Congressman who passed the pedophile bill who was one; or a fundamentalist preacher who was gay.

If you stop long enough to analyze another's life, you will see it.

See what?

A person's pain is his or her purpose. It is the devious or tricky nature of teaching humans. They only learn out of necessity so their pain is their mission, pointing them toward their life's goal. Because they hurt so much they have two choices, resolve the pain or let it consume them.

You're telling me that this is God's way. When we pray for peace, we get war?

I cannot speak for God. No one can. What I can say is that you are a soul; and as a soul, you are here to learn a lesson. You will not learn that lesson unless you are forced.

Why do I have to be forced?

You know the laws of entropy. You are pure energy and energy always moves from a higher energetic state to a lower energetic state unless there is a catalyst.

I get it. Tension is the natural state for growth and evolution. Where the tire from my car meets the road there is friction and that creates motion. If the tire spins in ice, there is no friction, and no motion. If there is not something creating resistance in my life, I will just sit there. Wow! I just had an interesting thought about pain and purpose.

What is it?

Does that mean that atheists are here to prove that God exists?

Now you're thinking.

✦✦✦

Day Six—

PURPOSE, CHANGE AND CONSTRUCTION

WHAT IS PURPOSE?

Is there a purpose to it?

To what?

Everything! Institutions, science, religion, my life, the planet, just everything! You have revealed so many of my flawed and outdated programs that I dare not attempt to answer my own questions because I am no longer sure of what I even mean by them.

Are you losing confidence because an old belief is being shattered or is there something you fear discovering?

It must be fear.

What is it that you fear?

Being wrong or touching the third rail!

What is it about being wrong that causes fear?

I don't actually know, but I have the strangest feeling that you just did it to me again!

What did I do?

You gave me this sinking feeling in my gut that something I have been doing or thinking is grossly wrong. It is about purpose—my purpose, your purpose, all the jobs I ever had, and all the projects I led. What if I was doing all these activities for the wrong reasons, and if I now understand the bigger purpose I...well I might just vomit.

Is this feeling a true pain in your gut, or is it mental suffering?

It is certainly not pain...and from what I learned before, I must say it very well might be suffering. If it keeps up for long I think it might turn into an ulcer.

Can you put your finger on the source of this suffering?

I think I just did. It is one of those assumptions, those programs about to explode. This program we are about to attack is about the purpose of everything. Our last conversation broke a few constructs that were deeply rooted, but this one—this one feels bigger.

Ah, an old belief then.

That's it! An old belief, you are about to expose an old belief as a fraud, and this fills me with fear.

What do you predict will be the outcome?

I think exposing and deleting this fraudulent belief about purpose will uninstall a program that will not only change my entire outlook on life, but all my behaviors! I might realize that everything I thought I knew was wrong, and everything I did was not for the reasons I suspected.

Could this be the essence of purpose?

What! Run that by me again.

Are you concerned that by understanding the essence of purpose, you might regret who you are or what you have done?

Clearly, that is the fear. No doubt about that.

No doubt, you say, but I do detect a semblance of doubt.

You are twisting my words! You do this often, but for some strange reason I find comfort in it all. I said no doubt I have a fear, but you imply I fear there is doubt.

Ha! You caught me. Forgive me, my friend.

What is there to forgive?

All this fear and doubt I have dropped at your feet.

Nonsense, this is all nonsense! Press forward and let's tackle this discussion on purpose while I have a moment of strength. You are my catalyst, and I need you to keep pushing me.

Yet, I fear there is little I can share with you about purpose.

Have I finally stumped you?

Indeed, it may be so.

At the most crucial juncture you are at a loss for words?

I know this saddens you, but I fear it might be true.

You have no fear.

How do you know?

I know you! You could almost say we are twins. We have been together forever. Never have I known fear to stop you from speaking or sharing your wisdom.

Then I have fooled you. I know nothing. And clearly I have no wisdom, and there is much I fear.

What! This is preposterous! You have helped me understand good and not-good, what makes things, and how I can send and receive messages. This is clearly wonderful knowledge and wisdom.

How can you say this is wisdom? How can you be so sure?

There are some things a person just knows. It is something you feel that is hard to explain in words.

Can you give me an example so that I may see and understand?

Well, indeed this is a pleasant turn of events. Allow me to gloat for a moment or two.

Take your time. I sense you enjoy these moments when I am at a loss for words.

Just a moment more…ah…this is wonderful.

I have all the time in the world. Literally.

Okay, I'm ready. Where would you like to begin?

In the beginning, if you please.

I suspect you know that the beginning of life is still in question.

Indulge me if you will: What is your belief?

What I know for certain, forget the books or classes, is that everything is energy. We already concluded that energy is not solid, as many mistakenly believe.

Is this an example of one of those items you just know but cannot prove?

Yes, it is.

What purpose does the energy of planet earth serve?

Surely you know this, everyone knows.

I would be grateful if you would remind me.

The earth is the source of minerals and resources. It provides the basic elements for everything we eat and use for construction.

Is there a word for all of this?

A word? Well, I never thought about it in that regard. Can you be more specific?

As the source of food and the provider of cement, what purpose does our planet serve?

It gives life I suppose.

Is it fair to say it serves to create?

Create, yes, I suppose that is one way to put it.

What else does this earth do?

I'm coming up blank. Help me out here, what are you thinking?

Expand your mind. If the minerals help create plants and materials at a micro level, what does the earth do at a macro level?

It is our foundation.

Are you saying it helps to support and sustain us?

Those are good words, yes.

Is the foundation upon which we stand always stable?

Absolutely not. It is always moving and shifting.

What happens to everything sitting on it when it shifts?

It gets destroyed.

I see.

The earth is also hot and burning inside, think of the core. It is a gigantic ball of magnetic fire.

Does fire serve a purpose?

Either you are humoring me or you have left your senses in some far off place today. Of course fire serves a purpose. It is the basic catalyst for manufacturing.

Then it also helps to create?

Yes, yes of course. But it also destroys.

Don't you burn wood to heat homes and cook food?

Yes, many still do.

If everything you say is true, then it occurs to me that fire, much like the earth, serves many purposes.

I see where you are going. We take it for granted, but the earth and fire give us life and create, as well as maintain and destroy. After all, the earth is dirt and the dirt is the source of the minerals for all our food.

Akara, ukara, and makara.

You said that before, I remember! What language is that again, and what did you say it meant?

It is Sanskrit. Akara means creation; ukara, preservation; and makara, dissolution.

I never heard of these words before you mentioned them.

You are a Christian, are you not?

Yes, but why would I know these words? Isn't Sanskrit a Hindu language?

It is.

Why should I know these words?

It is not the words you know, but their summation. The first letters of each of the three words form the syllable AUM.

A syllable? Go on.

You say it every day. AUM is the root of OM, which is the source of amen.

I never heard of A–U–M before, but I certainly know OM. This progression makes sense and if what you say is true, this means that every day billions of people from all walks of life and all religions are collectively praying to maintain the circle of life—creation, maintenance, and dissolution. And all of this is purpose, right?

Yes. This does make sense, doesn't it?

In what regard?

You told me that everything is energy, did you not?

I am not following you.

Can energy be created or destroyed?

You tease me again, but I will go along. Energy cannot be destroyed, merely transformed.

Can you now help me connect these disparate thoughts?

I believe that the purpose of all energy forms can be broken down into one of three objectives.

Please do carry on.

Yes. I see it clearly now. All energy serves three great purposes. The primary purpose is nothing more than the perpetuation of evolution, creation. The second purpose is that all matter co-exists to share energy and preserve the single system, maintenance. The third purpose is dissolution, when energy returns to its original root form and fuels the next transformation.

I see.

What do you think?

I think you got it.

Ah yes, one more thing. Energy does not do all those at the same time, my friend. It cannot be in three places at once you know.

I wondered when time would enter the story.

When will we tackle this issue of time?

Time and time again.

Okay, fine. Allow me to ask you a question.

Fire away.

Do you believe that time influences purpose?

Would that not be relative?

Possibly, but what would it be relative to?

The subject of purpose.

By subject do you mean the object, such as a person, company, element? Is this the subject of purpose?

Precisely. A noun. I will rephrase my question.

Please do, this is getting confusing.

Does time influence the purpose of a company or person?

Of course time influences companies and people. They all go through different stages of development.

Can you expound on the company as an illustration?

When a company is young and starting up, it must focus on creating its products and offerings. It may not have any time, energy, or resources to help the community.

This does indeed make sense. You of course imply that once a company has matured, it must then sustain the community or it will eventually dissolve.

I hadn't taken it that far, but I see your point; it must dissolve. If it doesn't sustain the energy in the community where it lives, then to prevent dissolution it will have to suck it out of another community. It cannot exist without energy you know.

To reinforce your point on stages of evolution, a company cannot do all those things at one time, but may over its entire lifetime.

Not may, it must!

That is a strong word. Why do you say must?

We have already agreed that energy must remain balanced. If one company, especially a large one, does not equally create, maintain, and dissolve, eventually there will be no energy for the rest of the system.

By system, do you mean the planet and community?

It depends on the sphere of influence of the company. It could mean the entire global ecosystem or it could mean the community in which the company is "living."

Does this mean that all companies eventually dissolve and are reborn?

All companies eventually transform, as do industries. Telegraph and telephone companies no longer exist but they have transformed into communications companies. Merger and integration is sort of nature's way of companies dissolving or transforming.

Is there a problem with this?

All energy is constantly seeking a higher state of evolution, the purpose of change. The only problem I can see is when the company or industry is artificially sustained. If it has passed its' useful life, it must be shut down or the evolutionary process will become imbalanced.

What does this mean in terms of a balance between the three great purposes?

All creation must be balanced with destruction as well as maintenance. Imagine if we as a species created more humans than the planet could sustain. The population would have to decline, or the species would have to find a way to live using less energy. By energy I mean power, food, air, water...all forms of energy.

Over time.

Correct. However, the time period is relative. For example a company may outlive its' useful purpose and cease to create value in five years or fifty years. Yet, it might take hundreds of years for humanity to create an imbalance with the air and water.

Are you saying that if there is an imbalance between man, air, and water, the system will react?

It's just a theory, but it seems completely logical to me that if humans disrupt the eco-system of the planet, the planet will fight back with storms, floods, and fires.

Are you still fearful?

That's interesting. It's gone.

What was it that made you afraid when we began the conversation?

I was afraid that when I discovered the essence of purpose that I would also discover that everything I did was without meaning.

Was it?

Actually quite the opposite is true.

How so?

I just applied everything I have ever done in my life with the energy industry, mergers and acquisitions, chaos theory, nuclear forces and my spiritual quest and pieced them all together.

Amen to that.

～～～

WHAT IS CHANGE?

We have talked a great deal about change, so tell me something, what do we mean by change?

What you perceive as change only takes place in the World of Form. In the World of Light there is no such thing as change because everything is a photon. If there were such a thing as a photon changing, it would be like a cancer cell attacking the very fabric of life. Everything would fall apart and the cycle of life would stop and you would truly be dead.

No such thing as change in a photon? Three days ago I would have said you had a screw loose...

I think you did.

...However, I do feel that change does exist.

What do you feel is an example of change?

When my body dies it turns to ashes. Is that not a change?

It most certainly is a change in form, but before we can agree on what is changing, we must first consider the viewpoint. From what perspective do you feel your body returning to ashes represents change?

From mine of course!

From what part of you? Your mind, heart, or your soul?

I never thought of it from anything other than just me.

Do you agree that in order for a change to occur, we must first agree on the object that is changing?

Possibly, but if you give me an example I can answer your question with more clarity.

Why not examine water, since the body is nearly three quarters water?

Water would be good.

What is the essence of water?

The essence of water is two parts hydrogen and one part oxygen molecules.

This you know how?

From science of course!

Science, I see. Now, how do you propose that water changes?

I think you must be going daft. Surely I don't have to explain this to you.

Humor me.

Ha! You use my own words against me, but very well. There are times when water is frozen and times when water is evaporated. Surely, you must agree that those are changes.

Not if I am a hydrogen molecule.

What! Run that by me again?

If I am a cold hydrogen molecule or a hot molecule, I am still a hydrogen molecule, am I not?

I am forced to agree. But I believe I have you trapped here. If you were once cold and now hot, indeed that is a change.

No, not if originally I was hot and then became cold and returned to my original hot state. In that case I have simply returned to my natural condition, and there is no change.

132

This is so easy! I love when I get to make my point. For once, I have caught you. You presuppose that you were hot and became cold. But what if you were originally cold and now became hot?

What we are debating is the original condition, are we not?

We are. But since we agree that water can be both hot and cold, it doesn't matter which condition you select as the original condition. I have you in checkmate.

Quite possible, but there is another condition, another reference point besides the original state which is under discussion. I wonder if you are aware of it.

What condition might that be?

Time.

Come again?

In order to decide whether there is a change in form, we agreed that we must have a change in reference to some original state.

Yes we did.

Must we also have a point in time for that original state?

I am reminded of our discussion on purpose.

Why is that?

I am starting to feel sick again.

Sick or not, you are the one asking the questions, and if you want answers you must see this through. Shall we continue or not?

Oh dear Lord…keep going.

Do you or do you not agree that the reference point for deciding if a change occurs must begin with a condition at a point in time?

Begrudgingly, I agree. Proceed, but I hope we are nearly finished.

Perhaps this will make you feel better.

Anything that makes me feel better would be an improvement.

If my original condition, born yesterday, was as a frozen hydrogen molecule, and today you boiled me until I evaporated, this would be considered a change in form.

I wish I had that recorded to mark my victory, but I feel it will be short lived.

But here is the determining factor: Is there any hydrogen molecule that was born yesterday?

You do this all the time, you know…change the rules of the game far into the discussion. We must stick with the molecule and drop this issue of time and birth nonsense. Everyone knows that hydrogen molecules are not alive!

I will ignore this question of life and death for the time being, and stick, as you say, to the hydrogen molecule. What is this molecule?

I am afraid you are about to outsmart me. As I willingly consent to these discussions, and I want to know the essence of change, don't stop. But please make it short.

Can we agree that molecules comprise protons, neutrons, and electrons?

Sub-atomic particles, yes. This seems to be our current understanding and, I thought, a point long ago resolved.

These sub-atomic particles may be further reduced to other, far smaller particles, which are currently referred to as bosons, quarks, and the like.

If this is going to turn into a lecture on physics I may have to depart. For the sake of our friendship, I will give you one more minute.

Allow me to simplify this by using the term "energy particles." Would that be acceptable?

Yes, press on.

Is it safe for me to assume that your earlier reference to your body dying is no different than the hydrogen molecule going from hot to cold to hot?

Stop right there! That is going too far. Those two are completely separate; you cannot make any such assumption! I will not allow it.

Separate in what way?

My body is alive and you cannot compare my body to the hydrogen molecule changing states because it is not alive.

The water molecule is not alive, you say?

Of course not! That's preposterous.

I assume you apply the same thought process to the minerals that are in both you and the earth. If they are in your body they are alive, but those not in you are not alive.

This is the first thing you have said today that makes complete sense.

So you believe you are alive even though you are made entirely of minerals and water?

We know that from science.

Where is the dividing line?

Excuse me?

Where is the dividing line, the location of separation that distinguishes between the living minerals and the dead minerals.

If they are in me, they are alive because I am alive!

I see. So when the water and minerals are excreted from your body then they are no longer alive, meaning they are now dead.

Yes.

What changed?

What do you mean by that?

Besides the fact that they were once inside your body and hot, and now are outside your body and cold, what changed?

Nothing. Nothing has changed besides these two factors.

There is one thing that changed.

What is that?

Time.

You see, I have you! Admit it! Your assertion that there is no such thing as change is completely shattered.

It is?

Yes, but I see you don't wish to admit it.

Admit what?

Admit that there was a change.

A change in what?

You said it yourself. They went from hot to cold and alive to dead.

Yes, indeed I did. Nevertheless, there is still a question of time. Was their original condition the time when they were inside your body, hot and alive; or was it originally outside your body, cold and dead?

My ashes. You are talking about my ashes.

Remember, man, that you are dust and unto dust, you shall return.

Ah, at last, I must concede because I see where this is going. My original, ageless condition is a soul, and the body was temporary.

To see no change in change is to understand the essence of change.

As crazy and confusing as that sounds, I think I get it. I see a change in the form, in my physical body, but that is not my original form. What then is the original form of me, and at what time?

There is no original form and there is no time. Photons don't have a form and they don't have a stopwatch. You are a light being, born in the World of Light, living in a shell, and returning to the light. This does not change.

My light body never changes?

Never.

What then am I, nothing?

Far from nothing, you are pure energy. How many different ways must I say this?

What then is the purpose of change? I mean, the change in form.

What you perceive as change in form is the energy flying about, seeking to gain more knowledge and evolve. As it is doing this you view it in the World of Form as building and creating; consuming and maintaining; dissolving, and beginning again. In the World of Form, this looks like change to you, but the energy photon never changes.

That's it? The essence of change is that there is no change, only the three great purposes: Creation, maintenance and dissolution. It's all about moving on to the next grade level?

Learning the differences between fear and desire or understanding the essence of love, virtues, and family is more than just graduating to the next level. But you must stop thinking that this all applies to just you, a man. I am talking about everything, the universe, galaxies, planets, trees, animals, and water. Man is not even close to a speck in the universe of energy.

WHAT IS CONSTRUCTION?

All this talk of earth, fire and water, gave me an idea.

What would that be?

Construction! All these planets and elements are all a part of one giant construction project. And the entire universe is constructed on four pillars.

You have always been fascinated with how and why things work. It's the engineer part of your soul.

Is that good or not-good?

It is neither, it is just part of your essence. However, sometimes you take this too far.

Why do you say I can go too far?

Remember your fanatical quest? The engineer inside is always trying to create a wiring diagram, and I am not extremely fond of diodes and circuit boards.

But diodes are very useful. They prevent current from flowing in more than one direction. If it weren't for diodes, current would flow in every direction and nothing digital would work. What do you have against diodes?

I have nothing against the electronic component, but I dislike people who act like diodes.

Oh. You're referring to people who are "One-Ways."

They are always there when they need you. The universe does not like One-Ways; such behavior goes against the universal laws.

Rest assured, in my thinking on construction, there are no diodes.

That would be a good thing. Just imagine if the wind were only present when it needed something. The earth might be somewhat irritated. If the earth was not pleased, she might vent her frustration on the water. Water in turn might call upon fire for assistance, and before you know it, the entire planet would be a giant inferno with intermittent floods.

That would be a travesty. But all forms of matter and energy are simultaneously connected in my concept of construction. This is the first pillar. Think of the planet as if it is the entire universe. We are connected through global supply chains, commerce, information flow, and the Internet.

I fear you must have been sleeping during some of our discussion. That, or I failed to discuss the virtue of humility.

I do not think I missed any salient points on virtues but I am quite content to sit here as your mind meanders through thoughts of separation, which is the second pillar by the way. Even though we are connected, we also are separate. Separate nations, companies, and ethnicities.

Funny you mention separation, for that is exactly what I was thinking about.

Perhaps it is a synchronicity?

I do believe you are playing with me. How did this occur?

I presume you are referring to the overlapping nature of our thought streams.

Is this another one of your four pillars?

Yes, this is the third pillar of universal construction. Knowledge and information overlaps: ideologies, ideas, thoughts, songs, and cultures, to mention a few

This is most intriguing. At some point in the last twenty-four hours your spirit has shifted.

Is it so hard to believe that all your lessons are rubbing off on me?

You appear to be tapping into the secrets of the universe without rational explanation. There can only be one way in which this has occurred.

What way would that be?

You have figured out how to see and hear into the source of knowledge and wisdom. There can be no other explanation.

Stop right there! I have sat here for a week as you have played and tormented me with some form of Socratic method. All the time I thought we were having a discussion. Turns out, it has been trickery the entire time.

Trickery you say, how so?

Whenever I thought I was following a stream of my own thoughts and ideas, you manipulated the discussion to help me realize the point of your pontification.

I see. I am a manipulator and pontificator now. I am sorry you feel it was trickery and manipulation. Forgive me.

You ask me to forgive you, then I do, and before you know it, I am caught in your web. I know where this is going, and I will not allow it to happen this time!

I believe what you are saying is that this is your information, your knowledge, and that some part of you will not allow me to partake in the discussion. Do I understand this correctly?

I understand the essence of the four pillars of construction, and it is mine to share. Not yours!

Very well. Share away, and I will remain here as a passive observer while you share your magnificent insights.

No questions?

No questions.

No forgiving?

No begging for forgiveness.

Very well. As you correctly surmised, I was playing with you.

Hmm.

Our thoughts do overlap. I already mentioned that.

I see.

Everything is likewise connected.

Am I allowed to ask questions?

You may. However, if you just relax I will explain it all without you having to exert yourself.

I never exert myself, as I prefer to remain in the flow and see where the light guides us.

How, one might ask, can something be both connected and separate and overlapping? Well, the answer is simple once you understand the big picture.

Simple…uh huh.

That is because of the fourth pillar of construction. Everything—houses, families, and nations—are interlocked.

Locked together? How so?

We are locked together with air, water, and minerals. The resources, the building blocks, are the greatest binding force. I'm not talking about the shape or form of the resources. I'm talking about the photons; the energy at a subatomic level is the light that binds.

It is simply amazing. The architect of this wonderful construct is indeed magnificent.

Thank you, but I'm not finished yet as there are two fascinating aspects to all this.

What are they?

If you try to pull one of the four pillars away, the system regresses and evolution goes backwards. The second point is that there is a fixed amount of energy! I am sure you remember our discussions on binding forces: Energy is finite. It cannot be created or destroyed.

Finite and binding. Yes I remember.

You have been saying it all along; we have to maintain the balance of energy. If we throw off the balance, the entire planet will react to restore the balance. Do you recall how energy was a critical part of all your lessons?

I do recall something about it.

Don't worry. You're not an engineer. It's difficult for non-engineering people to see the systemic view of such things.

Hmm, okay.

That's just about it. The essence of construction is four pillars; everything is connected, yet separate, overlapping and interlocked.

Is there anything else to your theory?

There is a postulate.

What is it?

If everything is connected, separated, overlapping, and interlocking, then all energy must maintain a balance between what we are creating and destroying.

Interesting.

Well, there you have it.

. . .

You have said hardly a thing this entire conversation. Are you feeling okay?

I didn't realize it was a conversation.

Of course it was!

Mm hm.

. . .

What's on your mind?

Diodes.

Why? I didn't mention any electronics.

I was thinking of the other kind of diode.

You mean the One-Ways? Always there when they need you?

The current that has been flowing from your brain and out of your mouth seems to have momentarily mitigated. Is there something wrong with your circuit board? Perhaps your transducer has surged and you need to check your fuse box?

. . .

Wow. How did you know that I was going to act like a diode?

Must have been a lucky guess.

You don't believe in those.

You say you understand the essence of construction, but your behavior demonstrates you do not. Shall I continue listening to your lecture on construction or just sit here and remain a part of the construct while you bask in your self-imposed World of Form, acting as if you are the be-all, end-all?

I am so sorry.

Please don't hang your head.

I just thought I had it! It came to me in a flash and I *knew* it was right and so profound and powerful!

It is profound. You did have a flash of wisdom, and it most certainly is powerful.

Why, then, do you diminish my accomplishment?

You are not taking this flash of wisdom and combining it with what we learned about purpose. Everything is a part of everything else. When a person or a company takes knowledge or energy and hoards it, claims it, or restricts it, that person is stopping the circle of life. Do you understand what I am saying?

You're telling me I was using this knowledge for myself, to make myself feel good. When I do that, whether it is with money, resources, or a company, I am in essence depriving everyone else of their rightful energy.

Exactly! Your understanding of the essence of construction and the four pillars is beautiful, but you have to understand that it's not yours.

Why did I do that?

You arrogantly presumed that ancient knowledge and wisdom was yours and yours alone. The ego is a necessary part of construction, but you must not let it take control. If it does, the essence of human life will ultimately be destroyed because the World of Form will consume everything.

Day Seven —

LOVE, WAR AND SEX

WHAT IS LOVE?

What is love?

I was wondering when you would ask this question.

Why is that?

We've touched on it many times.

When was that? I don't remember talking about it.

Love is the primary mover.

Love is the primary mover? I thought the mind was the primary mover?

What ever gave you that idea?

I read it in a book.

That book is sadly mistaken, and most likely written by an atheist.

Why would you say that?

What is an atheist?

An atheist is a person who does not believe in God, of course.

Why would someone not believe in God?

Perhaps it is because it is not in their belief system, meaning they did not have parents that believed. Or perhaps they went to a school where religion was not taught or…

…Excuse me, but what does religion have to do with God?

Are you kidding me? Why would you ask such a thing?

I see we must have a long discussion on the essence of religion. Never mind for now, we shall come back to this. For now, keep telling me why an atheist doesn't believe in God.

It boils down to everything we talked about in belief systems.

Is it safe to assume that the primary educator of belief systems is usually a parent?

I think teachers play a big role, but yes, parents are the primary educators of beliefs.

Could not the best, most well-meaning teacher be overridden by the lowest of parents?

I think so, at least during the early years of life. Why do you ask?

What is it that someone who cannot believe in God is most likely missing from his or her parents? Something their parents did not teach them?

Given how we got into this subject, I have to assume you are referring to love.

What would a person's life be like who has never known love or experienced love?

I think they would feel very lonely and isolated, which would make them depressed and possibly volatile.

How would someone who does not know love likely respond to external stimuli, events, and people?

You should ask a psychologist as I am practicing without a license. If I must guess, I believe they would tend to live toward one of two extremes.

What are those extremes?

One extreme could be a solitary life so they can avoid any relationship that might cause pain.

What is the other end of the spectrum?

I think they would go deep into their mind, using logic and formulas, and spend most of their life trying to either prove the existence of God or the non-existence of God.

Why would they do this?

It's their pain! We said that before. They have to find an answer: It is their only way to remain sane and not bounce to the other extreme. Clearly if there were a God, they would have to conclude that this God must be a terrible and mean God because as a child they were not loved. They would look at all the words and teachings about God—love, compassion, generosity—and say, "That's not the God I know! He must not exist!" I don't even think it would be a conscious thought.

You may be correct, then again maybe not. Give me an example of the middle.

The middle is a person who doesn't have to be on a search, or living a solitary life. They might be waiting for something to come along, to push them to one side of the fence or the other. You know, real or not.

Have you ever heard how some atheists use logic to deny the existence of God?

Tell me.

They conclude that if there is a God and God is good, as Divine Providence tells us, then clearly God must not exist since the world is full of pain and suffering.

They can't do that!

Do what?

Atheists cannot use the existence of God to deny Him. It's a paradox. Since they see not-good things happening, this is their proof there is no God. Their logic only works by assuming there is a God and God is good.

How true. One cannot accuse someone of doing or not doing something, if that someone does not exist.

Precisely. It's a paradox. I think they feel this way because they do not understand the essence of pain and suffering. It is only the behavior of men that is not-good, not God.

Perhaps they have not paid attention to synchronicities, signs, and truth bumps.

What do those have to do with anything?

How many years of such phenomena did it take for you to believe?

. . .

Are you okay?

Oh no. This is terrible.

I feel it. I know. Take your time.

I am, but I am about to cry.

It's okay.

It took me seven years, or more, and I still didn't believe. I did not truly believe until I spoke to you.

Now would be a good time to go into your heart and give thanks.

I can't right now…I am too consumed with what just struck me.

…

I did that.

What?

I used my mind and went on a search to prove or disprove the existence of God.

It's okay.

I thought I was a Christian, but I wasn't.

Crying is good.

They are tears of joy, and…I don't know how to describe it.

Peace?

I was an atheist! I didn't feel loved. I felt abused and abandoned, and I retreated into my mind for more than a decade. Then all these signs and interventions brought me back from the brink and I had to go on this quest! Oh my God! This story is about me!

Now now, it's okay. This is a beautiful moment.

I…I feel as if a great burden has been lifted, and I understand why I went on this quest.

What does that feel like?

Peace, tranquility…I am at ease. A huge burden has been lifted from me, and I…I think I have completed my quest.

Why are you in tears?

I am so happy! All of those phenomena came from God. He was helping me.

Why would He do that?

He loves me.

Why would an atheist make such statements? Why did you go on your quest?

The answer is the same, I didn't feel loved, and neither do atheists.

What then is love?

Love is the opposite of what an atheist believes, and that is God. God is love.

～～～

WHAT IS WAR?

My trusted companion, there is something that has been on my mind and bothering me for many years.

What is it that troubles you so?

I want to understand what is war.

War is the outward manifestation of inner turmoil. It is the battle for love.

Why do we choose to destroy each other in lieu of the inner demons?

Consider the essence of battle itself. Would you agree that the first requirement is opposing sides?

I have to agree.

Would you further agree that once we have opposing sides we must also have a domain in which to fight?

If by domain you mean a field upon which we do battle, be that physical or virtual; yes, that does make sense. However, I think there is another critical requirement, and I am uncertain as to which precedes which.

What is this third requirement?

We must have something we are waging battle over! It could be an idea, territory, asset, pride, ego, or as is sometimes the case, a beautiful woman.

The items you list, may I label them as attachments?

You may.

We now have opposing forces, an attachment upon which to disagree, and a battlefield. Once we have weapons, are the most important elements all in place?

We could debate this for more time than the sun has left in the day, but my stomach is persuading me to concede and move on.

It has been said that the second rule of battle is to know thy enemy. What then is the first?

It must be to know thyself.

Why would this be true?

In terms of the battle and primary elements, if you are to succeed, you must know your military advantage. This means you must know both your weaknesses as well as those of your enemy.

Military, why did you say military?

Are we not talking of war?

Forgive me—I thought you meant another kind of war.

What other kind of war can there be?

I was under the impression that we were discussing the war within.

I was thinking about the war with, you know, missiles and bombs.

Aren't they one in the same?

Of course they aren't. My internal war was a war between my mind and my soul. I discovered it had nothing to do with religion, science, or my desire to understand how phenomena work. The battle inside me was the atheist paradox: I was loved but didn't feel loved; therefore I couldn't believe there was a God. I think that ultimately, all internal battles probably boil down to a fear of not being loved.

Why aren't internal and external battles the same?

The weapons in the external war are missiles, bombs, lasers, and the like.

What are the weapons within?

The battle within takes place at a cellular level, and as I said, the primary battlefield is between the head and the heart. That means the internal weapons are thoughts.

How does the essence of a thought differ from the essence of a laser weapon? Didn't we agree that a thought was in essence a photon, an energy particle?

I never thought of it that way. I guess there really isn't much of a difference between a thought photon and a laser photon—except, I suppose, the target.

How do the reasons for the outer war differ from the reasons you mentioned for the inner war? Are they not both a battle over love and fear?

Now that you mention it, I am not sure they are different. After all, the reasons I mentioned for my war are the same reasons men wage external war: Lust, greed, jealousy, ego, and assets. They all boil down to a reaction to not being loved. The opposite of love is in essence fear. Not hatred.

Are you sure about that?

I'm not sure about anything at the moment, which is why I am questioning everything! Think about it, a not-good warriors' fear is that they are not loved. It could be the woman that left him or her, the home that was taken away, or the parent that didn't want them. Outwardly they appear angry, which turns into hatred and then fighting but inside it was all a fear; a fear of being alone, abandoned or not loved. That emptiness transforms into anger, which morphs into hatred, and that creates a monster whose only purpose is to force others to pay attention and show respect and fill its broken heart.

Are we in agreement then, that both the inner and outer war have battlefields, similar weapons, and similar motivations?

I agree with you, they are similar.

What about the attachments? How did the battle between your mind and soul over attachments differ from the attachments in an outer war?

I'm not so sure they differ either. In the final analysis, I think they are all about ideas, which originate from beliefs and are reinforced with faulty or outdated programs.

Yes indeed, they are one in the same, and when you felt unloved as a result of these limited programs, you went too deep into in your mind, subconsciously seeking to be loved; which is of course the answer to your question.

The answer to my question! Are you saying the mind's desire to be loved is the essence of all wars?

Did you forget what God is in such a short time?

God is love, but why would God create wars?

Why indeed? It certainly would support the atheist paradox. He must be a mean and terrible God, must He not?

I know this in my heart not to be true.

Then feel into your heart, why would God not eliminate wars? What have we learned from wars?

Pain and suffering.

The battle within, yes?

Yes, the battle created in my mind from the World of Form and the associated confusion.

Were it not for this internal battle, where would you be?

Trapped in the World of Form chasing attachments and ignoring confirmations and signs.

Where are you now?

I am in my heart.

Why?

It is peaceful, and I am loved. Why would I want to be anywhere else?

So why is there war?

War exists to inspire humanity to find love.

Now tell me, back to your earlier question: Why do people choose to fight each other instead of attacking the inner demons?

That's easy: If I accept that the problem is me—all the faulty and outdated programs, all the pain and suffering, every argument or accident—then I can't blame my problems on someone else! I have to accept personal responsibility and that's a lot more work.

How true.

I just had a thought about all the top graduates I know from the military academies. They never do this.

Do what?

Blame someone else.

Why is that?

They accept personal responsibility and as a result, they are all very balanced and spiritual people. In fact many of them became religious or spiritual leaders later in their life. The same is true about the Navy SEALS I know.

What is it they know that you now know?

They know that death is an illusion. They believe in God's love. They are not fighting for territory or attachments.

What are they warriors for, if not for attachments?

They realized, far sooner than I did, that all wars are a battle for love, and that internal battle is expressed outwardly in our environment. The only way external wars will end is for all warriors to realize they are loved and have always been loved.

WHAT IS SEX?

Since we are tackling all the big ones today, we may as well try to understand the essence of sex.

How would you like to begin?

I always prefer to start in the beginning with the big picture.

And what would be the beginning of sex?

I believe we touched on it in the discussion on war.

Are you talking about love?

Actually, I was thinking about the inner turmoil, the battle to find love, and all the crazy external things people do along the way.

When a person does not have someone they truly love, they will somehow find a way to have sex.

I suppose in that regard we are no different than the average creature.

The average creature, indeed. A crocodile, for example, is a mere reptile whose brain is so small it has no thoughts and only a few instincts.

What are they?

When a crocodile sees something moving, it either wants to eat it or have sex with it.

They do have rather small brains.

Small or not, they seem to be using it wisely.

You do have a point. Why waste limited mental faculty on something as mundane as admiring the trees or the lake?

Indeed. It is a jungle you know. Survival is at stake in the jungle.

Is this not the essence of sex? Reproduction?

I think you have it! It must have been another irrational thought of yours.

Irrational, eh? I think you meant that it was a moment of inspiration. Calling it irrational seems to diminish the beauty of it all.

The beauty of what?

The beauty of my inspiration that the essence of sex is survival, reproduction, continuation of the species!

Oh of course. How silly of me. I thought we were talking about reptilian creatures with limited mental capacity. And yet they know about the circle of life. Forgive me for calling it irrational.

We have had a long day. You *did* help me understand the essence of love and war.

Perhaps you are correct. Love and war did take a lot out of me.

It did require a great deal of energy.

What required a great deal of energy?

Waging war and making love…I mean, discovering you are loved. Excuse me. I think that was a Freudian slip.

It was probably an unconscious thought. You know, something you were suppressing. All the talk of the reptiles reproducing probably provoked it.

I think you're right. However, my new understanding of the ability of my mind to create confusion and my knowledge of all the faulty and outdated programs does make me wonder if somehow my mind was subconsciously taking me back to the question at hand.

Taking you back, what do you mean, taking you back?

My question, have you forgotten it?

No, you wanted to know what is sex.

Yes, that is why I was suggesting we get back to it.

What do you think we have been talking about?

We've been talking about reptiles and reproduction, of course.

Isn't this the essence of sex?

Well, I suppose it is part of it.

What would be another part?

I was thinking about making love?

I do say! Although we are close friends, you are not my type.

I didn't mean together!

Ha! This I understood but I couldn't resist the temptation. What was it you were saying again?

That part of sex is about making love.

Love? Love, you say? We finished the discussion on love did we not?

Well, yes, but this is a continuation of the discussion.
Did we not conclude that God was love?
Yes.

So why do you bring up the question of God and sex? You've lost me completely.

I was trying to say that one of the reasons a person has sex is because they are in love and they want to have a family.

I have said this once and then twice and cannot believe I must say it again: Where do you come up with such ideas?

What is it that I have confused this time?

Sex is nothing more than an act to perpetuate the species, a simple reptilian response.

Are you trying to tell me that sex and love are completely different?

Of course they are different. Do you think a crocodile makes love? Does he bring flowers over to the lady crocs, sing, and dance for them? That only happens in Disney films. You haven't been watching those have you?

Ha! That's funny. No, I don't think crocodiles make love.

They also don't make war.

What's that?

They don't make war.

Why is that?

We just finished talking about war and you think that crocs make war?

You mean to say that crocodiles don't make love because they don't make war?

You have it backwards. They don't make war because they have no need for love.

Why would that be?

They are not subject to the mind and ego trying to overcome faulty programs.

Oh I get it now, they don't have an ego, and therefore no internal turmoil that creates an external war.

Precisely. They're reptiles. Reptiles have sex, which is completely distinct from love.

~~~

Day Eight—

Form, Reality and Truth

What is Form?

You have referred to "form" many times, but I don't know what you mean.

What do understand it to be so far?

You said form was all the raises I wanted, branded shirts, fancy cars, watches, and big houses—all the objects I desired to buy, sell, or hold—for the purpose of gratification and pleasing my senses.

Yes, this is true. Don't stop.

I can understand how I became addicted to these things, and that was not-good. But does that mean all form is not-good?

The World of Form is the physical construct in which your light body exists when you are human, and these objects are neither good nor not-good. However, some of the people who believe that the World of Form is the complete reality use form to control and dominate others. That is most certainly not-good. As form did with you, it does with them: Feeds the senses, strokes the ego, and creates attachments that result in suffering.

If the World of Form creates the attachments that make me suffer, that means it also creates the faulty and outdated programs that confuse me, correct?

Yes. The people in this world create these programs to explain their façade, and they use them to perpetuate the illusion.

What then is the World of Light that you keep talking about?

It is the energy, the Source, God. The World of Light is the essence of your soul and all matter, physical and non-physical.

If the light is love, why would I want to live in the World of Form? It makes no sense to me.

Only your mind wants to live in the World of Form, and it wants to live there forever.

Where does my soul want to exist?

Your soul knows what you are, where you came from, and that death is an illusion. The soul knows it is from the light and happens to be in a body in the World of Form but it chooses to live in form to mature.

Does the World of Light exist in the World of Form?

Now you are talking about the nature of reality, which includes both realms. They are inseparable. Go back to our box example. The World of Form is the box and this box exists inside the light. The beings in the light see both the outside and inside of the box. Outside the box is the home of God, spirits, guardians, and angels. It is the source of all inspiration, inventions, knowledge, wisdom, confirmations, and interventions.

This is all a bit confusing.

Thinking. Ah yes, that necessary faculty in the World of Form that is at times valuable. I do believe this is the realm where arms and legs exist as well.

Why are you bringing *that* up again?

I am trying to help you connect our lessons so that you can see your true nature. Your soul and everything in existence outside the box is the World of Light, where there are no arms and legs, no minds, and therefore no thinking. Arms are only manifest inside the box, in the World of Form.

I am feeling very confused.

The form, your mind, it is resisting. You are blowing up the illusion that it is in control, and it is attacking you. It doesn't want you to do this.

I'm getting very agitated. I'm starting to twitch. It feels uncomfortable. How do I stop it?

Write down the opposing truth. Do not write the problem, only the solution.

What's that?

Write and say, "I am a light being. My soul is in charge. I am safe and secure."

I am a light being. My soul is in charge. I am safe and secure.
I am a light being. My soul is in charge. I am safe and secure.
I am a light being. My soul is in charge. I am safe and secure.

Do you feel better now?

Yes. Thank you. I feel…relieved! There was a battle going on between my mind and soul, but after I acknowledged my soul it…well it is as if it erased the outdated thought in my mind.

Tell me, where do you prefer to live, I mean right now?

Why, the World of Light, of course!

Really? Outside the box? How can you live there?

I just came from inside the box, and it was nothing but a pale grey world of schematics, formulae, circles and squares, corners and angles, and a thousand people begging and coercing me to believe their version of truth. You saw what just happened, my mind was fighting for control! Why would I want to return to the World of Form?

Return? My dear friend, you never left. You are still inside the box as we speak. You only had glimpses of outside the box when you drowned and went through the tunnel. You had another experience when you broke your neck, died, and left your body. Every time you traveled through the Gateway, or left your body you were outside the box. But you are still in form and that is inside the box.

Are you telling me that the only time I am not in the box is when I am dead? Sorry, I mean my physical body decays and my soul leaves my body?

You know this. Don't ask me; tell me, who lives in the World of Light?

Only souls live in the World of Light, where they no longer have a physical form. I call them angels, saints, guardians, or the deceased. Is this correct?

Yes, so what do we call a soul who, such as yourself, realizes they are in physical form but from the World of Light?

They are people who know and understand the light, so I would call them Believers.

Very good. Now tell me, what are the beliefs of the Believers?

They exist in a world of unlimited potential where ideas are the will of God and divine inspiration.

Carry on.

They are an instrument of God's will, using hammers and saws to do only that which is good. Their world is filled with synchronicities and truth bumps pointing them on the Way. The Believers know that God is love and that war is the raging battle between a mind that believes it exists to conquer the world and a soul that knows otherwise. Do I have it right?

Yes. The mind loves the math, science, manufacturing and selling so it can control and master. The soul however, knows that the reason for living in form is to experience the pain, suffering, and confusion, so they can learn compassion and forgiveness, generosity, and eventually love and self-mastery.

As strange and paradoxical as this at first appears, it is exactly what happened to me. Anyone who wants to heal simply has to record and listen to their own ranting to know what's wrong with them.

When they do heal, does this make them a master of others?

There is a huge difference between helping a person achieve self-mastery, as you have done with me, and saying you are my master.

What is the difference?

A person can only be the master of his or her own soul. I believe when they achieve this level they become a Believer, a light warrior. But that does not mean a warrior is, or ever should be, a master of others. Only people stuck in the World of Form, Not-Yet-Believers, try to master others.

Well stated indeed. A true master knows he is not anyone else's master. People who do not recognize this are individuals who have not yet discovered the light.

WHAT IS REALITY?

I would like to have a debate.

What do you mean by debate, are we not already debating?

Yes, but this one is different. I propose something more like a battle over a subject that is long overdue to be slain.

What subject is that?

I would like to battle on the subject of reality: What is it?

What a fantastic idea! Since this is your chosen confrontation, you may choose the battlefield.

I choose the field of energy.

Very well, then I shall choose the weapons and I choose photons.

Shall we choose sides?

Indeed.

Which side would you like to represent?

I will represent the World of Form, and I will fight for attachments, materialism, domination, and control!

Perfect! I will represent the World of Light. I fight for love, sustainability, and unity!

May the Light be with you!

And may the institutions on Madison Avenue and Wall Street be with you!

I say, before we commence fencing, where do the realms of science and faith stand on this field of battle?

Is this important?

I must know, and I presume you as well, if either of us may rely upon these philosophies for ammunition upon the battlefield.

Your point is well taken. Since I am new at fencing with photons, what is your suggestion?

I believe they must remain neutral, like Switzerland, as they have a stake in both sides.

Does that mean we may use their territory or must remain clear?

Good question. I suggest, as with all sides that choose to remain neutral, the battle itself will determine their fate.

Very well. They shall remain neutral for as long as possible.

I say, I detest delaying the commencement but I have another thought that might be most relevant.

What is that?

Do we need a judge? If we do not have judges, who shall decide if my attack is valid or off-target?

Clearly, you are experienced in fencing. We must have a judge. My suggestion is that the judges be Prudence, Temperance, Justice, and Fortitude.

Use the four cardinal virtues as judges? What a wonderful suggestion. However, it might be wise to have an odd number. We don't want a tie you know. Why not add Perseverance, and then we shall be ready to commence.

I concur. I do believe we have established all the boundaries except one. We have an idea, a field, weapons, sides, constituents, and judges but we have yet to agree on the means of determining the victor.

I believe you are correct; otherwise, we might be fencing this bout for all eternity. I believe this is the final point.

Points! Why I think the Light just inspired you with an excellent idea. We shall use points. I propose the first to win three touches is the victor.

Inspiration from the Light, you say? Why, it was nothing of the sort. It was my superior mental intellect and knowledge of fencing.

En guard you heathen, for the source of all ideas and inspiration is God, not man!

Is this then your first attack, that of ideas and inspirations?

Does your mind have difficulty accepting this fact! You are nothing without the ideas generated by the World of Light, nothing!

Your ideas are worthless without my hands and intellect to turn them into reality!

Your reality is nothing but your realm of toys, money and factories. It is disgusting how you fondle your meaning-less possessions! All you do is lust after things to please your physical senses!

…Temperance says I just struck you right between the eyes. One for me!

If it weren't for my physical form, your ideas would have no useful existence and they would be nothing but photons floating in space.

…Justice says he agrees on the grounds of reasonableness. One for me!

Attempt to use justice on me again and I shall parry and riposte straight to your heart. Oh, wait a minute, how silly of me! Programs that promote nothing but division and separation don't have a heart! Your ego has done nothing but destroy the environment and squander our natural resources as you seek more and more of what you want with no comprehension of what you need!

...Prudence says that careful and considerate management of finite resources is indeed a necessary factor and has awarded me a point! Two to one!

You have fallen victim to your own private world of illusionary photons without comprehension of the nature of industrial, social, or cosmic evolution! Why if it were not for man's countless trials and errors, there would be no change. Without change, there is no growth, and without growth we would never have even conceived of photons, time, space, or matter let alone the essence of your World of Light.

Fortitude is shouting from the bleachers at the top of his lungs, "Yes, yes, it takes strength and courage to forge the laws of evolution," and it is now two to two!

Calling upon science in your defense? A little early in the match, isn't it? You must be desperate. I knew you could not stand long without the weight of science to support you. Fear not, my soul mate. In your final hours of battle my heart is open, and I understand your clinging to science. Rest assured you are a soul, and after our bodies are slain we will not rot in hell. Hell is but an illusion created by non-Believers who seek to recruit you through fear.

I see Perseverance is about to call the match! Three to...

Put your hands down, Perseverance! This match is not over until I riposte. You dare to call upon the concepts of religion? Stand by, for I am about to fleche!

A running frontal assault! Bring it on! If I only saw your limited World of Form I might be frightened, but since I also see the World of Light I know death is an illusion and matter is not solid. I call upon the Grace of God and dematerialize myself! Go ahead, sprint and lunge at nothing whenever you feel strong enough!

Now it is you who calls science to your aid. The almighty denizen of the World of Light must rely upon an explanation of matter and time to shield himself from my blade. Ha! An admission of defeat!

I see Perseverance is standing and about to raise her hand and award me the final point…three to…

I think you need glasses: She is raising two hands.

Two hands. How could that be?

It is a tie.

The World of Form lost? Oh my, now I shall rot in hell.

The World of Light didn't win? Dear God, where were you?

We did all that for a tie?

Hold on, I think there *is* a winner.

Which, form or light?

Switzerland.

It's neutral. Doesn't that mean it is a draw?

That means reality is a duality of form and light.

No, if reality were a duality that would make the essence of living a competition, in which case it would be a tie and the World of Form would win by default.

Why would they win by default?

The Not-Yet-Believers are stuck in the concept of separation; the Believers know we are one. If living were a competition then, by definition, it is a world of separation. Do you agree?

I see your point, and I absolutely agree. There is no such thing as a tie or even a competition. The appearance of a duality between form and light is an illusion.

The essence of reality appears to be a duality, when in truth it is a non-duality, comprising Believers who understand the "light in form" and those who are Not-Yet-Believers existing in form.

❧❧❧

WHAT IS TRUTH?

What is truth? After all these discussions I am so confused by all the conflicting information. I no longer know what to believe.

I see your point. If you knew the truth, then you would not be confused.

That's right, and it would make me feel better.

How then do you determine the truth in light of so many conflicting influences?

I don't know.

Yes, you do know. You have always known.

What have I always known?

The truth.

According to whom?

My dear friend, you have always known your truth according to your values, perceptions, experiences, physical and mental abilities, ideologies, and memory.

Are you saying that what others think is true, is not important?

No, I am saying that what you think is true is more important.

I don't see the difference.

There is a huge difference.

I don't see how.

Maybe you should spend some time in silence and figure it out for yourself.

...Are you thinking?

...

Yes.

Day Nine—

Science and Religion

What is Science?

All of these thoughts about God, intentions, good and not-good, energy…they make me wonder: Where is the dividing line between science and faith?

Dividing line? Why do you insist on creating these artificial separations? We just agreed life is a non-duality; there is no dividing line. Science is a form of faith.

Blasphemy! God is either going to strike me with lightning for asking the question, or you for confusing science with faith. I prefer to think it will be you. However, given my close proximity, I might become collateral damage!

Why would God strike either one of us for sharing the essence of science? He is the greatest scientist of all.

God? A scientist? I can hear the uproar now. If you keep up with this heresy I shall cover my ears.

Heresy! If you dare to doubt the scientific gifts of God then it is you that will be struck for it is you that blasphemes—not I.

Why I subject myself to this ridicule I don't know. Here I thought we could have an interesting conversation about a topic I hold dear. But somehow, I find myself accused of blasphemy! What a twisted soul you have. I should have been the wiser since you have done this to me many times in the few days we've been together.

Together, what does that mean?

Together, as in sharing and exchanging information, what else could it mean?

Forgive me, I gave you credit when credit was not due.

What did you give me credit for?

Never mind, it does not matter, you didn't understand and it is my fault for making such an egregious assumption.

What assumption did you make?

I assumed you spoke of something more philosophical when you said we were together, that is all. I was mistaken.

I think this a ruse to shift the discussion, but as things have calmed down and I am no longer in danger of becoming incinerated, I will play along with your musings. Besides, I know very well what you were talking about. I just wasn't inclined to go there.

Where was that?

I was referring to our togetherness of course. Why, has your mind wandered? I was speaking of something very profound.

Me? Lose that which is profound? I don't believe I would. How is it insightful that we are together? It seems rather casual to me.

Ah, now I understand.

What is it that you understand?

You are subjecting me to faith.

Why do you assume I am not subjecting you to science?

I spoke of causality, the principle of cause and effects, the lightning, remember? I'm sorry it was lost upon you. I promise not to make any further presumptions, or to guide the conversation in too technical a direction.

Now it is you creating a diversion, pretending to know of cause and effect. Why, if you knew what I knew about the essence of science, your binding energy would become so excited you might fly apart at the seams and be nothing but floating particles.

You prove my point! It isn't possible for me to come apart at my seams and fly around the room! If somehow I did rattle the binding energy that holds my physical matter together, I would not "fly around." I would collapse into a pile of ashes.

Physical matter? Is that what you are, physical matter? Here I thought as a nuclear engineer you knew something of physics and fusion and the laws of nature.

Are you implying that I am not physical matter and that if my electrons became excited I would simply dematerialize?

If I were a man of science, such as you, I would never believe such nonsense.

Do I feel vindication?

I believe what you feel is the force of gravity, but who am I to know for sure since I have no idea what that is.

It is a force, described by one of Newton's laws.

A law is it now?

It has always been a law.

I thought it was a postulate, you know, a given, an assumption made that fits within observable behavior but has never been proven. I am sure you understand the difference between theories, laws, postulates, and givens.

...

Why do you look so pale?

I know very well the meaning of these terms but I must also admit that science has not been able to prove why gravity is what it is.

My friend, it is a small technicality; do not be concerned. I am sure there are many small things yet to be worked out by the great scientific minds of your generation. It is merely a coincidence that I chose gravity. Look at all the great knowledge and discoveries about big things in fundamental physics or all the small things in theoretical physics! My gosh, humanity is on the cusp of great discoveries!

...

Is that a frown I see? I thought I was conceding to your superior intellect, so why are you now frowning?

I don't know whether this is trickery, brilliance, or a synchronicity, but I know for certain it is no accident or coincidence.

What is the synchronicity?

That you should bring up the two major branches of science—the theory on big things in fundamental physics and the study of small things in theoretical physics—in this context.

Why does this catch you as a surprise?

I must inform you of a small problem between these two branches of physics.

Do share so I might learn.

Fundamental and theoretical physics are both correct and provide demonstrable results in their own domain; however, they are completely incompatible with each other.

When you say incompatible, what does that mean?

It means, for example, that one is like a MAC program made by Apple, and the other like a Windows program made by Microsoft. They do not work on the same equipment or in the same operating system.

Does that mean they are both wrong?

No.

How would you describe them to a stranger?

I would say that both are useful, but both are incomplete.

Well, complete or incomplete, these two branches of physics are surely useful and demonstrate the ingenuity of humanity! Why, mankind has sent people to the moon and decoded the human genome. Surely these are wonderful accomplishments.

This is absolutely true. Look at how we are capable of reproducing the healing power of nature in all our synthetic drugs, and we can genetically modify food to increase production per acre of land.

Yes indeed those are significant and practical accomplishments. Actually, I was thinking of scientific knowledge that is even more rudimentary; man's understanding of the sun, the source of life, force, or fire, the basic catalyst in all energy and manufacturing.

Yes, humanity certainly has come a long way in our under-standing of science. I see your point. I shouldn't fret that these two branches of physics are incompatible.

Let us not concern ourselves with the complex nature of cause and effect, or the nature of time, purpose, intentions, or those soft and intangible matters such as love, feelings, happiness or health. Humanity must first understand the universe before it can begin to understand man.

...

I say, you have really taken a turn for the worse. Your face looks so pale. Is there something wrong?

My friend, I cannot lead you astray. Science knows noth-ing of those basic human needs or the essence of the sun or fire, or even "spooky behavior", otherwise known in physics as quantum entanglement. Why, for centuries we thought the sun was burning. How ludicrous is that?

Why is that ludicrous? It looks like it is burning, after all.

Fire requires a few basic ingredients to sustain it, and one of those is oxygen.

Yes.

There is no oxygen in space.

If science has laws that accurately enable us to send a man to the moon or predict gravity and force, why can't it explain the source of gravity, quantum entanglement, or the essence of fire?

Perhaps we do not try. I don't know.

Not try? Why would science not try?

After living with your spouse for thirty years, you stop seeing what once was clear. I believe the same thing happens to scientists who have lived with theories for hundreds of years. They forget that the theory has never been proven and, even in light of blatant contradictions, they cannot overcome their blind spots.

Faulty programming.

Faulty programming that perpetuates outdated beliefs! Until someone, who has no such blinders, sees what is clear. These people are sometimes called Nobel laureates. This is why all change in the World of Form is a series of slow incremental changes, followed by radical revolutions. Eventually a big program is exposed as outdated, faulty, or both, and institutions, companies, and beliefs drop off the flat earth.

What are these scientific assumptions fundamentally based on?

...

Oh my, are you all right? Don't fall over.

I am okay now, thank you. I just got a little woozy.

What caused that?

I believe it was a disturbance in my field of energy. Something major was being blown away from every cell in my being.

What would that be?

Another illusion was just shattered! Science and faith are not separate; in fact they could not be more similar!

Now it is you that blasphemes! Science is based on methods, theories, practices, and more importantly, repeatability, is it not?

Indeed it is. However, the foundation of all modern science is based on a set of laws, and as you spoke I came to realize that these are not laws at all. They are all assumptions, and we haven't the foggiest idea why some of them work. We can prove what happens *when* they work—Newton's laws on gravity or force, for example—but we cannot explain *why*.

What is the terminology your generation would use to describe a collection of people who share a like set of methods, principles, and theories based on unproven laws?

I would probably call them people of faith.

~~~

WHAT IS RELIGION?

I see you have recovered quickly. In fact, you seem happy. To what do we owe this jubilance?

It was our discussion on science. I had a realization: There is a religion called science, and knowing that fills me with peace.

A religion called science, why would this realization bring you such peace?

All our lives you have known me as a nuclear engineer, a math major. However, there is something I have never revealed to you before, and I am excited to share it with you today.

I cannot wait. Hurry now, before the moment is lost.

As a young adult, I dreamed of becoming a priest.

A priest? Really! How fascinating.

When I was on the submarine I was actually the lay minister, and I conducted services.

What other deep secrets are within?

It has always troubled me that there is this separation between science and faith. Our battle over reality and discussions about the World of Form and the World of Light has helped clarify something for me.

Tell me about this clarification.

There is a religion called science. Once scientists accept this fact, they will be more at ease. It struck me in the middle of the night when I woke up startled.

What startled you from your slumber?

It was a dream.

I love dreams. Tell me about yours.

I was standing on what appeared to be a large volcanic rock a few hundred yards from the shoreline. It was dawn and the sun was just peeking over the horizon. In front of me there was a steep, vertical cliff and oceans of tantalizing blue water. The waves were gently sliding over the rocks. I looked down at my feet and saw a dark round hole in a rock. A large brown and green snake came slithering out and wrapped himself around my legs. I stood there, unafraid, and watched this coiling serpent as it slowly moved up my body. As it reached my chest, it stretched out in front of me, turned pure white, and then began shedding its skin.

What a wonderful dream.

What does it mean?

A snake is a powerful sign not to be feared. It is a symbol of healing, spiritual awakening, and transformation.

I see now. This is why I feel peaceful. I am beginning to fully accept the realization that I came from the World of Light and I live in the World of Form.

That is wonderful.

It's strange for me to think this way. In general, science doesn't believe in miracles because it cannot explain them, yet on the other hand, science believes in gravity and it cannot explain that either. Then I asked myself, what is the difference?

Indeed, what is the difference?

That wasn't rhetorical. I want to know, what is the difference? If science is in essence a religion, what is religion?

Did it ever occur to you that there might also be a science called religion?

What a wonderful thought! I think you are onto something here. Since I believe that God is the greatest scientist of them all, there must be a science to explain miracles. Why shouldn't science be the essence of religious practices?

Are you saying that the essence of fire, the burning of incense, the flow of water, and frequencies created by chanting have some deeper scientific meaning?

This is why you need a man of science by your side. Everything is energy, and all of these physical activities change matter at a subatomic level.

Has science proven this?

Time and time again.

Do you think that the wise ones of the past, the founders of all modern religions, knew this?

They certainly did not know the science, but they must have recognized that there were some physical effects that resulted from saying prayers, singing chants, or people laying hands over the sick. Why else would every major religion include these kinds of activities in their rituals and holy books?

What else do all religions have in common?

Every religion also has just about the same cardinal virtues. You know, similar philosophies about love, compassion, not-good thoughts, and attachments.

Why would they have all this in common?

I don't know. It never really occurred to me, but now that you ask, I suppose one might call these religious postulates.

Help me understand what a religious postulate might be?

A religious if-then statement.

What are some examples of religious postulates?

If you ask, then you shall receive; if you give to others, then you are giving to yourself; if you do good things to others, then good things happen to you.

Wonderful! Any others?

If you love your neighbor as yourself, then he will love you in return.

Have these passed the test of repeatability?

Oh yes, only millions of times over hundreds of years. Clearly, more testing and research must be conducted.

What I think you are confirming, from your scientific point of view, is that the assumption that religion is a science has validity.

Yes, don't you see? These are the postulates that dictate the laws of synchronicity and support what we said about intentions. Not only that, but it confirms what we know about the actions of photons and spooky behavior.

How would you structure religion in a scientific model?

Religions have sets of principles, terms, practices, and postulates that are the basis for their behaviors. As with science, not all can be proven, but there is overwhelming evidence that when a practitioner follows the commandments, meaning the postulates, and follows the religions practices, the desired results are achieved.

What about the World of Form and World of Light? How do they fit into the model?

The World of Light in scientific terms is called a photon and in religious vernacular it is the kingdom of Heaven.

Why haven't other people thought of this?

I interviewed many of the world's top theologians on my radio program, and I was shocked to hear them tell me that there really is no commonly accepted global definition of what we mean by religion.

Really? No common definition?

Allow me to explain. Some believe that religion is a collection of belief systems. Others say it is a set of practices and cultural norms. Still others say it is all of these and more, including a philosophy, virtues, or divine laws. Do you see my point? Is it some of these, all of these, or none of these? If it is this entire list, then religion is everything! The very fact that we muddle all this together and then have furious debates means that we do not agree on what we mean by religion.

The meaning is simple. How could it elude your generation of great minds and scientific thinkers?

Are you saying *you* know the meaning of the word religion?

It's elementary. Take it apart and examine the roots.

Re-lig-ion.

What does "re" mean to you?

To repeat.

What does "lig" mean?

Nothing in English, but the roots go back to Christianity and the basis of that is Latin, so I assume the Latin meaning would be best.

What is that?

The word "lig" in Latin means "to bind."

What does "ion" mean?

An ion is the basic building block of all matter. It is the essence of a molecule, with either a positive or negative charge.

Positive or negative you say.

Yes, why?

Positive versus negative. I am reminded of up versus down, left versus right, good versus not-good.

I see your point. These are all opposing forces, but one without the other cannot exist.

Put them all together and what do we have?

The essence of religion is a science. This science is the study of the circular and continuous evolution of forces that bind all of life and living. Religion exists to maintain a balance between opposing forces to sustain the evolutionary cycle.

What happens if re-lig-ion fails to fulfill this purpose?

The opposing forces will be out of balance, and the natural circle of life, the evolutionary cycle, will be broken.

Is this not the understanding of your generation of religious leaders?

No. Sadly, I think some of them might have it backwards.

IS RELIGION GOOD OR NOT-GOOD?

I am not sure if you are attacking science and religion or supporting them?

Neither am I.

Very well. How should we proceed?

If there is no object that "is" not-good, then religion must be good. If so, how?

Many people find comfort, peace, and love as well as a realization of God due to religious institutions.

I agree. If it weren't for religion, how would most people learn about the World of Light? On the other hand, do you agree that many wars and terrible deeds have occurred because of religion?

Any objective observer would agree on this point. However, we did say that there is nothing that is not-good, only people who do not-good things. By virtue of this, I would say that religion is by definition good, but the people who seek to dominate and control the World of Form may use religion as their spear. This would be not-good. Then again, didn't your search for truth begin with suffering? Your own battle with domination and control? Didn't we agree that your purpose is your pain?

We confirmed this as a truism. In fact, there appears to be a law that the way to finding one's true calling and purpose is through pain and suffering. It is through pain that we learn forgiveness and compassion, generosity and finally love. If it applies to me individually, it might apply to us all collectively.

Then there is the issue of love and war. Did we or did we not agree that the essence of God is love, and that the purpose of war is a means to find God's love?

Yes we did. We also agreed that external war is a manifestation of an internal battle and that the two have much in common. We agreed there is no such thing as the devil or evil and that all things, no matter how terrible they may first appear, do in fact result in something that is good for all of humanity. It's just that not everything terrible is good for each individual.

I do believe that the existence of the concepts "devil" and "evil" promotes fear and division, and this is counter to God's love and message of unity. Perhaps it is time for modern religious leaders to reevaluate these concepts.

Based on the definition we created for religion I would absolutely agree. All religious institutions have an important role to play in maintaining balance in the circle of life. And religion is intimately tied to the three great purposes of creation, maintenance, and dissolution.

AUM, OM and Amen. It appears we have reached a consensus: Religion is good but the actions of individuals who use religion as a spear to control and conquer are not-good. The role of religion is to maintain a balance between the World of Light and the World of Form.

IS SCIENCE GOOD OR NOT-GOOD?

Since we've challenged the essence of religion, I feel it is only fair to do the same with science.

You mean that we should address the question of good or not-good?

Yes! And if you recall, I have experienced several miracles in my life. First, I was told on numerous occasions that Archangel Michael saved me from dying.

I remember.

I also had that experience with my neck, and although Eastern medical practitioners and Western medical practitioners have differing beliefs, there is no doubt in my mind that the healing of my vertebrae was indeed a miracle.

I concur that being saved from drowning, breaking your neck, and the healing of your neck are all miraculous events.

Yet, I feel these events are explainable. What does this mean?

It is, in my humble opinion, the responsibility of the realm of science to use modern knowledge and technologies to analyze, document and explain miracles and similar events.

Agreed! Science has documented the mind-body-spirit connection for many years, but it seems that the people that have this knowledge are afraid to share it.

It has, and they are afraid, just as you were. However, religious organizations cannot share the mind-body-spirit connection because they do not understand the science.

I remember our discussion on matter. We said that science has sufficient evidence to substantiate the power of our thoughts to manipulate reality at a subatomic level and to prove the way in which miracles are performed. If there are stakeholders that are preventing science from sharing this knowledge, that is certainly not-good, and completely at odds with the essence of science—which by the way, comes from the Latin root scientia—meaning knowledge! I feel strongly however, as do you, that it is incumbent upon science to approach religion and jointly share these kinds of stories and open a global dialogue. After all, it is the scientists who have the knowledge of most scientific studies, not the clergy.

I agree. However, are you telling me that I have to accept that institutions as powerful and wealthy and organized as religions do not have the means and wherewithal to educate their own cadre of scientists?

Your point is well taken. If there are religious scientists they must have the ability to conduct mind-body-spirit research and document the cause–effect relationships.

Where are we then? Is science good or not-good?

It is the same as always: Science is good. It is only the actions of individuals who limit or manipulate knowledge for the purpose of controlling others in the World of Form that are not-good.

DAY TEN —

LIFE, LIVING AND KNOWLEDGE

WHAT IS LIFE?

I do enjoy all this jousting on lofty subjects. I would say these moments are the essence of life.

What do you mean by the essence of life?

It is a saying: The life of the party; you know, joyful, fun, the meaning of life.

You must be more careful with your choice of words. Having fun is not life. It is living.

Hmm, if I examine the fact that life is a noun and living a verb, I believe you are correct. Jousting, playing, dancing, singing, and working are living, not life.

What then is the essence of life?

That is an interesting question. I believe we agreed that I am a soul in a body, from the World of Light, living in the World of Form. Reality is a non-duality, neither man nor

God, physical or spiritual, but a combination of the two. What then is the essence of life? And how can I even evaluate the question since I'm in the box?

What box is that?

The box. I am in the box of form. How can I possibly understand the World of Light when I am inside the box? It's like the people in the Dr. Seuss story that live in Whoville.

What is the relevance of Whoville?

The people of Whoville thought they lived in a large world, but in reality it was very tiny, the corner of a snowflake. We are not so different. Humans are specks on a planet that is a speck in the Milky Way galaxy, which is a speck in a universe filled with billions of galaxies. As I can see the snowflake where the "Who's" reside, I'm able to see the true nature of their lives, but I can't leave the World of Form to discuss the essence of my life from a point in space.

The answer to the question lies in the question itself. Begin by understanding what you mean by "life"?

Excellent point! Is it your opinion that life comprises things that are either alive or not alive?

That would depend upon…

I know, please, do not say it…time. It would depend on time, which we have yet to discuss.

I was going to say it depends on how you define the boundaries of the box. What life is to a tree is not life to God or a star.

Since I am neither a tree nor God I will pass on the relative comparison. However, when I attempt to see through the eyes of God I think I am able to better understand life.

I believe we are beginning to define a set of criteria from which to evaluate the subject. Please continue.

Can we agree that life, from a point of view in space, does not have anything to do with time, temperature, breathing, national origin, gender, or sexual preference?

I can agree with that list, but you must add political ideologies as well.

You are joking aren't you?

I am not joking. How would a lifelong member of the Sierra Club react if we defined a tree as the essence of life and they were unable to use this definition in the World of Form?

I see your point. Just think how the Republican Party would feel if all of a sudden we declared that oil was alive and that burning it was akin to murder.

If you do not exclude political ideologies from our search for the definition of life, you very well may come up with an incomplete definition. After all, you know how divisive abortion is. Just think of the complications if the Supreme Court had to decide the point of conception for a drop of oil.

We would have to stop burning oil, and what about the trees? Did life begin before the seedling fell to the ground or after it germinated? We might have to stop cutting down trees if we declared they were an essential part of life. Which is funny…because I think they are an essential part of life! After all, they do provide oxygen.

And just imagine what might happen if we brought water into our definition of life.

I never thought about that. What if we concluded that water was life? Would we have to stop drinking it?

Water is life and that is exactly why you drink it! Which is precisely why you cannot evaluate the essence of life from inside the box, as you so correctly identified. It traps you in all the contradictions and illusions of the World of Form.

Yes, I know. The World of Form certainly has created a great number of artificial definitions of what is alive and what is not–alive. So how do I proceed?

I will repeat what I said before; the answer to the question lies in the question itself. Now what is the essence of life?

Now I think I see your point. I was assuming that life was alive, but that notion came from inside the box.

Precisely. Take a position from outside the box, the point of view of God and your soul, and now ask yourself to define this object you call life.

It has to be something that is common to everything and everywhere, a shared characteristic.

Here and beyond this planet as well?

Everywhere, which means it doesn't need to have eyes, a mouth, or a brain to be alive, does it?

No, life doesn't have to have eyes, ears, brains, noses, or mouths. I'll also add that I don't think it has to breathe, digest, excrete, or reproduce.

If that is the criteria than it is really simple.

How so?

There is only one thing I can think of that fits the criteria.

What?

Energy.

The essence of life is energy, as in photons?

It's perfect. Life...what I am calling photons...exists in the World of Form but it comes from the World of Light; it never dies; it is always creating, maintaining and dissolving; it is the essence of God and us, with no mouth or clothes. Energy is all these things.

Are you saying that energy is both the form and the light?

Absolutely. For an object to have life, be life, or be alive, all it needs is to be receiving and transferring energy. And everything is energy on this planet and in space.

Your soul agrees.

~~~

WHAT IS LIVING?

If life is pure energy, then what is the essence of living?

Why do you ask this question?

I think it is a very important question. The more I think about it, the more I believe it is one of the most relevant and important questions of all. We have spent our entire time talking about things that happen in a life, to a life, and the purpose of a life, but we haven't spent any time talking about the process of a life, what "living" really means!

That's funny; I think that is all we have been talking about.

Do you mean that all these experiences are the essence of living?

Were these discussions not the summation of your life?

Not all of it, but yes, a great deal. Whoa, hold on a minute! Are we talking about living in the World of Form or living in the World of Light?

That is a good question. As I am an innocent bystander in your World of Form, and it is your question, you tell me.

It has to be both.

Why?

We just agreed that the essence of life is energy and it exists in both realms, so living has to be the same definition whether I am inside or outside of the box.

That is quite interesting. Are we now once again discussing the question from the point of view of God?

We must. The essence of living must include living in the World of Light, a place of no-time, no death, no space, no—anything but light.

And God does not have arms and legs.

Or a political agenda, meaning His viewpoint on the process of living cannot involve any form. I know this is confusing. Heck, the question even confuses me. So let me try to explain very clearly. To define life, we were both inside and outside the box of form, right?

Correct.

Well to define living we must do same thing. The question must be evaluated not only from the realm of God, but also from the viewpoint of the World of Form. The definition must include not only the objects in form—jobs , cars, and promotions—but also everything *experienced* in the form.

What do you mean by experienced?

I mean the essence of living must involve pain and suffering, joy and love, and of course living and dying!

That is The Way, of course.

The what?

No, The Way.

What way?

Not what way, The Way.

Which way is that?

It isn't a direction.

If it isn't a direction, are you saying it is a destination?

The essence of living is not a destination.

Is this a riddle?

What I am telling you is that the essence of living is The Way and yes, it is similar to a riddle. The journey is confusing and unique to every person both in body and spirit.

You're saying we all have to pass the same tests and learn the same lessons, but we do it in completely different ways?

Now you see where I am going. This journey can be as gentle as a flower or as violent as a volcano or both.

I see. And as it was for me, it can be elusive and endless…

Or it can be seized and achieved.

I can take it, but I cannot give it.

You can use it, but you cannot own it.

I can learn it, but I cannot teach it.

It can be courageous or timid;

Exhilarating or boring;

Joyous or tearful;

Loving or fearful;

Understanding or spiteful;

Greedy or generous;

Inspirational or petrifying;

It can be none of these things…

…Moreover, it can be all of them.

This is the journey…

The Way is the process of living, in form and spirit. It varies from soul to soul, object to object. How each person experiences The Way is intimately linked to one's life purpose in physical form.

It is the essence of living, from all perspectives, in the box or from a star.

You get to decide how the journey begins and ends. It serves one purpose...

Wait! I know this; it is for me to discover my purpose, my essence in this lifetime, and to grow and evolve as a soul.

This is The Way, the essence of living in both the World of Form and the World of Light.

〜〜〜

WHAT DO I KNOW?

I find it amazing to think that I have gained all these insights in such a short period of time. In fact, the more I learn the less I feel I know.

What have you learned?

Everything is pure energy; my brain is a thought-generating and sharing computer; my intentions create either a world of fear or love, and nothing is an accident. Shall I keep going?

Reality is a non-duality, death is an illusion, matter is not solid, and the concept of time changes everything you thought was certain and how you interpret events.

But The Way, that is most enlightening. It is so simple yet it appears so complex. If you view it all from the form, it is easy to see how we created all these words you called silly—coincidences, accidents, death, evil—but from God's point of view, it all makes complete sense, and all the contradictions evaporate into thin air.

Why is The Way so enlightening?

Because it is The Way that is the secret, the great mystery—our pain is our purpose and God doesn't have pixie dust. It's actually humorous when you think about it. The tests and trials we must pass to arrive at enlightenment are fixed, but the sequence and the means by which we check them off is completely elastic. It is completely in our hands.

Living in the World of Form is merely the instrument through which you experience the trials and tests.

That leaves me with only a few more questions.

I thought we were finished. What other questions do you have?

I have to review what I have learned.

Who are you?

I am a father and a husband, a son and an entrepreneur, a corporate CEO and a submarine officer, a television and a radio host, a writer and a man of science, a warrior and a philosopher. I am all of these and none of these.

How can you be all of those and none of those?

I am all of those in the World of Form, but I am none of those in the World of Light. I am a light being, a soul. The people who live in the World of Form believe we must all compete and conquer. I allowed them to fill me with faulty and outdated programs that contradicted themselves at every turn. They caused me to become confused and suffer because I forgot who I was and from where I came. You have helped me realize this, and I am most grateful.

Why are you grateful?

It is because of where I came from and where I return to, the World of Light. You helped me realize that before I was blind, but now I see. I no longer see suffering; I see a person growing. I no longer see evil people or institutions; I see not-good behaviors. I no longer see change; I see evolution and growth. I no longer see coincidences; I see synchronicities. I see and understand all this because of you. All that you helped me learn brings me peace, so I am grateful.

Why are you here?

I am here to learn, to grow, and to evolve. In doing so I achieve a higher state of awareness.

If that is who you are and why your soul is here, why then are you here, now, in this body and in this life?

I think you mean my purpose in this lifetime. Is that correct?

Indeed that is what I mean.

I am here for many reasons, but my purpose is that I am a communicator. I receive information from both worlds. I talk to enlightened beings such as you. Then I share that information to help others however I can.

You are here to help other people see the form so that they too might see past the façade and experience the World of Light.

How do I do that?

Help them see their true self. Show them The Way as you experienced it.

Teach them to be authentic and transparent?

Help them find the light within and without.

It sounds honorable.

It is noble.

What else do I need to know?

The Way, the truth, and the light are all there is to know.

Day Eleven —

DAY, TIME AND ILLUSIONS

WHAT IS A DAY?

I understand my purpose is to help share my story. I had to go through so much suffering to get to the point where I was ready to ask the questions I've been asking you. How do I help others to see what I have seen?

How about picking something everyone understands? Something like, "What is a day in the eyes of God?"

You honestly believe that is something everyone thinks about?

I didn't say they think about it. I said something that everyone can understand.

Oh. Sorry, you did say that. But how could I possibly know the answer to this question?

Perhaps you do not know what it is, but you know what it is not.

I do?

Tell me what you know and don't know about a day from God's perspective.

I know that Genesis says that God created light on the first day, but he only created the Sun on the fourth day. If there wasn't a sun or a planet until the fourth day, I know that Genesis could not possibly refer to one "earth" day.

We agree that Genesis isn't talking about sunlight.

Correct. No sun, no planet, therefore no sunlight.

What makes you say we are not talking about earth days?

Clearly without a planet or sun, a day in the eyes of God could not be twenty-four hours.

What if God lived on Venus where a day is almost six thousand hours? Could this be closer? After all, it would give God more time.

True but we have the same problem as the planets and the sun didn't exist. Besides, it is 460 degrees Celsius on Venus. That's 860 degrees Fahrenheit.

I see your point. It sounds more like Hell then Heaven. Maybe God lives in the center of the Milky Way Galaxy. Do you know what a day is in the galaxy?

We define a day on earth as the time it takes for a planet to make a complete revolution on its axis. As far as I know the galaxy isn't a planet and doesn't have a sun in the middle, so I don't believe it can have a day.

True, but if you tried to define a day for relative comparison, how would you do it?

I understand that the Milky Way Galaxy is 27,000 light years across from one end to the other. It would take a very long time for something that large to rotate. Just think of a very large Ferris wheel. If it rotated too fast, the kids would go flying out of their seats.

Let us then assume for the sake of discussion that the Mayans had it right, and the galaxy makes a complete rotation about once every 26,000 years.

Isn't this getting a bit nebulous? That's a bit of a hazy estimate.

Hazy it may be, but it does make more sense that God would live in the middle of a galaxy then on a planet. In addition, if he lived in the middle of the galaxy it would mean that God created the world in seven galactic days, which would be closer to 182,000 earth years using our nebulous estimations.

It is beginning to sound more reasonable. Yet, it does leave the universe as a follow-up problem.

In what regard?

God would still be in a box.

Ah yes, the box of the galaxy.

We are making so many assumptions here, the foremost being that God has to live anywhere. Perhaps he lives everywhere and nowhere.

There is no question that time would be relative to the location of God.

Would that be east, west, north, or south of me? Are we talking about the Julian calendar or the Gregorian calendar?

Here's another one: How far away are you from God?

You are making my point. We absolutely must determine the reference point relative to the planet in order to know what this could mean.

Why on this planet?

Time in space is completely different. All I care about is my planet.

It is true that speed and gravity affect time on every planet. Time on the moon or the satellites is not the same as earth time.

I think I understand why you feel this question is a good place to start.

Why?

It points out the obvious contradictions and assumptions that God lives in one place or that a day is twenty-four hours. I have to conclude that God does not have a watch.

It is essential to understand that the essence of a day in the eyes of God impacts everything you have come to believe in the World of Form.

I thought this was a very strange question. However, I have to admit I could never have predicted the questions or discussion we had over the last ten days, so I just trusted your guidance on this one.

Now that we know that God does not have a watch, it is time to tackle the relevance of time itself.

⌒⌒⌒

IS TIME RELEVANT?

When you said let's talk about the relevance of time, did you mean why time matters or if it matters at all?

I mean both. In one way, time does matter, but only as a unit of measure for man in the World of Form. On the other hand, God does not have a watch. From the omnipotent point of view time is irrelevant. It does not exist.

It is the primary unit we use to measure everything in the World of Form, but I don't understand why it is irrelevant to God.

If you think about all of your suffering you will recall that time is the source of all the confusion and suffering in the World of Form. In other words, time is the source of all the great illusions that plague humanity. The concept of death is a result of time.

You mean the death of my physical body is the result of time.

Please think about what you just said. Does your soul die?

Oops. No.

The concept of all death is the result of time. Time made you believe that there is such a thing as change. The concept of time changes your beliefs and your point of view on history.

Time is so deeply rooted in my supercomputer that I have a hard time wrapping my arms around this notion of no-time.

Am I safe in saying that from the World of Light, we agreed there is no-time?

I am fine with that.

Consider it then from the World of Form and your five senses. Can you smell time?

That is a good one. Let me think, can I smell time? I can smell my mother's cooking even though she passed away two decades ago, but that is not time. It is a memory. No. I say no.

Can you see time?

I can see the leaves falling from a tree and the vision of my watch sinking, but this is a result of what we say happens in time, not an example of time itself.

Can you hear time?

Not unless it is that song, "Time in A Bottle," by Jim Croce.

Can you feel time?

I don't think there is a single sense in the World of Form that allows me to define this concept called time.

There is one thing you can do with time.

What's that?

You can measure it.

We said that before. It is the only thing I believe it is useful for, measurements.

Correct. It is a manmade construct devised to help explain the experiences or elements of the Form. Perhaps it would help if you applied this sensory test to other scientific constructs, such as gravity, mass, matter, or temperature.

I do hope you are not going to ask me twenty-five questions, I don't think I can sit here that long.

Very well. Clearly gravity and temperature can be felt, yes?

No doubt. Matter, velocity, and mass can be felt, and I can see them.

Yes, although you might encounter some resistance in attempting to explain how you see or feel velocity, but I do understand what you mean. You can see things moving at different paces.

We could spend a very long time doing this with all sorts of examples, but I would like to suggest a theory if you will, not proven of course, but something that might accelerate our discussion on time.

What is that?

If time is the only scientific term that cannot be detected by the five senses, *then* time is an arbitrary unit of measure. I can see and feel the *effects* of what we call time, like aging, but that is not time.

Why do you say arbitrary?

Is it five yards to the kitchen, five meters, or five miles?

I think you mean five minutes, five seconds, or five hours to the kitchen. That would depend upon whether you were walking or running.

Blast it, you shattered my postulate!

What's the matter? How did I do that?

Matter has nothing to do with it; it is distance and speed. You found two more components that cannot be detected by our senses. Hold on, let me check…smell, feel…I do believe that time does not appear to be a bachelor.

It's a threesome, time, distance, and speed all dancing together?

Indeed, a ménage à trois of sorts.

Yes, but who is courting whom?

This might have been why we stumbled on velocity. In order to determine who is courting whom, perhaps we need to consider their relative positions. You know, who is on top of whom?

Oh no, I think we have another friend who joined the party.

A foursome? What do the French call a foursome? Who is the uninvited guest?

Location.

Ah, yes, location…is another relative term. You don't see location; you see a house or a tree. Some people feel a location, but it is not the location they feel but the energy of that location. Location is another relative term based on my position. If we keep this up, we might discover the secret to dematerialization.

What do we now know, and how did we arrive at this place?

We have time, speed, distance, and location as a collection of amorphous but relative lovers that cannot be detected by any of our five senses and as of yet, we are not sure who is doing what to whom or what the French call a foursome.

I see. How, again, did we arrive in this place…or perhaps I should more appropriately say "no-place" and in "no-time"?

We found ourselves trapped here by attempting to nail down time. I…oh my! I have it.

What?

You just defined the World of Form. Think about it: What is form but what we perceive to be a three-dimensional object in the fourth dimension of time-space? We just said that none of these terms—time, speed, distance, or location—could actually be sensed. They are all artificial creations to sustain the World of Form. Without them, the Form falls apart and is exposed.

It's bigger than that. What are you forgetting that was created in the World of Form that caused you to become confused?

The programs.

Yes, the programs. All of your beliefs are grounded in the World of Form and artificially sustained by manmade constructs that feed your senses. The elimination of time, speed, distance, or location obliterates your outdated and faulty programs.

Yes, I see it now, all of it in fact. I recall you said something to me about time when I was talking to you about programs. What was that?

I asked you how you got all these outdated and silly words. What made you believe that who you are is what you do, or that life is a destination stop at retirement?

I said it was the media or culture, but you said it was older than that. You said it went back to the dawn of time.

Do you see now? Do you understand?

I think I do.

Tell me.

It's the Original Download you mentioned. You didn't mean the beginning of Earth or civilization, you literally meant the dawn of time, the birth of the construct called time.

What has this construct created?

The World of Form, all the illusions and words to describe things that otherwise would not make sense: Death, evil, suffering, coincidences, miracles, there are dozens of them! In order for this façade to make sense, we had to create all these terms and words!

Make sense to whom?

It would not make sense to the senses, the five senses.

Nevertheless, there are more than five senses aren't there.

Yes, there is a sixth sense.

What is that sixth sense?

I believe it is our ability to feel and understand the light, God.

Love.

So the greatest illusion of all time is time itself. Without time, these concepts and constructs fall apart.

The light does not have a stopwatch, only form does.

There is no death. We said that many times, but then you hammered it home when you said the concept of time created the concept of death.

Time is nothing more than man's way of talking about what passes, transforms, and changes in the World of Form. Humanity has confused itself in all aspects of life by focusing on the five physical senses and then creating an artificial construct to make the form seem real.

WHAT IS GOD'S GREATEST
MODERN CREATION?

Now, I have a question for you. What is God's greatest modern creation?

That is a very interesting question. I'm not sure, but I have a feeling you are going to help me discover it.

We just agreed that when you shatter the illusion of time, everything in the World of Form falls apart. Distance and location become irrelevant and time shrinks. Does this remind you of anything in your life?

Oh, yes! I used those very words from 1999 till the present day to describe the effects of the Internet.

Why do you use these words?

Thanks to fast and cheap technology that connected the world, production cycle times shrank to nearly zero and created an interconnected global community. In less than ten years, almost half of the Fortune 50 companies that existed in 1990 were gone. Entire industries including music, publishing, automotive, energy, banking, and real estate underwent an unprecedented evolutionary shift. Software products such as SAP, Oracle, and JD Edwards connected every division and function in every nation, allowing them to move operations to the least expensive location. Global business lines were consolidated from hundreds to just a few. In the process, these companies formed global hubs and gave birth to outsourcing and off-shoring, setting the stage for India to become a world leader in outsourcing and China a world leader in manufacturing.

Is it safe to say that time, distance, and location became irrelevant in this Internet age?

Oh, yes. And that enabled three billion Asians to be connected to the western world of shopping and debt. The result was a sudden explosion of human consumption that drove a ten-year instantaneous and unsustainable burst of economic activity.

What else did it do?

It awakened the world to knowledge and wisdom and created a financial crisis, energy crisis, and the Arab Spring. Which in hindsight, I would say is God's means to "level-set" the entire world.

If you could see from the eyes of God, why would the Internet be the greatest invention of all?

God is proving the essence of construction; everything and everyone are connected yet separate, overlapping, and interlocked. This theory applies not only to people, but also the natural resources. God is waking up the world and showing us the true nature of reality. He has forced us to become consciously aware of just how dependent we are on each other, and...I think He is also showing us how insignificant our little domains and fiefdoms really are.

There are no accidents.

No coincidences.

There are just confirmations and synchronicities.

I have a thought and it's a big one.

What is it?

I think that a very big shift is occurring, and although everyone feels this, few have concisely defined this change. We all share a sense of unease, and whatever this shift is, it's creating a great polarity. The pace of change in the World of Form is accelerating, and the shift is pulling us together and simultaneously pushing us apart. That's what I mean by the polarity.

That is why the Internet is God's greatest modern creation. It is the great equalizer, leveling knowledge, wisdom, wealth, and power around the world.

True! But part of the problem is that some individuals are in fact inhibiting or blocking the Internet.

This is because those powerful individuals are trying to stop evolution. They must not be allowed to block the free flow of information.

They cannot stop it. That is like putting a lid on a pot of boiling water. The tighter you clamp the lid, the greater the pressure gets until eventually it explodes. People will no longer stand by and allow the few to control the many. The ideas that long ago created and perpetuated a false reality and sustained repressive environments are being obliterated by the Internet.

Very true. But what precisely is the heat source that is making the water boil?

Now that is a great question. Let me think…whatever the heat source is, it is the source of the tension creating the polarity in the world.

If humanity is being pulled together, on what are people collectively converging?

I think we are converging on the illusions and contradictions. That's it! The world is awakening to the illusions in the World of Form! This shift in thought transcends time, location, religion, national borders, governments, and is tapping into the soul of every man, woman, and child.

What is it that is pushing the world apart?

The people in power that are living in the form, trying to maintain control!

You now know the forces and reasons for the polarity, but you have yet to define the point of contention. What is the single point of friction?

On a personal level it is the battle between mind and soul.

How is this personal battle being fought globally? How is it manifesting?

The world is being called into the light and those who wish to remain masters of men and conquerors of the world refuse to let go of control. In doing so, they are sustaining all the crises. They refuse to let go of fossil fuels and exploit free energy from the vacuum of space. They refuse to let go of their pills and procedures and embrace the healing power of light. The Arab Spring is that part of the world shifting their thoughts and fighting for their spiritual right to be free!

What institutional terms would the world use to describe the mind and soul?

Is it science and faith?

Yes, the global shift is the convergence of science and faith. Tens of millions of people around the world are awakening to the realization that these two terms are one in the same subjects but are seen differently when viewed from inside or outside the box. The Internet has helped the world to realize that you are all one, not just in form, but also in light.

I understand now. There is only one inevitable conclusion from our discussions about matter, life, living, planets, the entire ecosystem, and the web.

What is that?

There is no such thing as separation.

~~~

THE LAST QUESTION—WHO ARE YOU?

Today is our last day and I have to be getting back to my memoir. You have asked me a lot of questions, and now I have one for you.

We have talked about everything under the sun. How could you have any more questions?

Who are you?

Pardon me?

Who are you?

What a silly question. I am you.

How could that be?

I am you, you are me, and we are one.

I…I don't understand. You have helped me learn things that I didn't know or understand. You have shared knowledge and wisdom I did not have. How could you possibly be me?

Think about the lessons on souls, time, reality, change, God, and the World of Light. I am your light, your inner self, the observer, the guide, the true you, your soul, I am your life force. I am all of these things.

How did you find me?

I didn't find you, you found me.

Where are you?

I am everywhere and nowhere, I am here and beyond, above and below, no place and everyplace.

You are the light aren't you?

I am, and so are you.

Somehow, I knew that. Deep inside, some part of me is at peace.

We are one, indeed, but not just you and me. Everyone is a part of the light.

Everyone's thoughts, feelings all wrapped into one. It makes sense. Does that mean you are God?

No.

Why not?

I am a part of God and God is a part of me, and you, but that does not make you or me God.

Why not?

Your planet is just a snowflake.

～～～

EPILOGUE

THE WAY, THE TRUTH AND THE LIGHT

I set out to write a memoir. After four months of writing and editing, I was exhausted and confused. A friend told me about a spiritual program that helps people focus their thoughts and energy, and so I went to the class. After the class my mind was suddenly very clear, and I was filled with an overwhelming sense of peace. A few days later I opened a new blank word document, and I started writing a journal to myself. It was a dialogue with an unnamed person. As I wrote, I had no idea what was going to come out next. Who this unnamed voice was, I did not know. All I knew was that I couldn't stop writing. When the story was complete my wife asked me what I had written, and I told her I didn't know. I hadn't read it yet.

"How could you not know what you wrote? You wrote it," she said.

"I may have written it, but I really don't remember but a few words."

The book literally continued to write itself as a dialogue between two friends, and I, the writer, was the observer. Whenever I stopped to read what I wrote, the World of Form got in the way and told me to stop, trying to confuse me. I decided to shut off my mind and just keep writing. Even after I'd finished writing the conversation and was ready to hand it off to another set of eyes, I still wasn't ready to define the unnamed participant. I was fairly certain that I was the one who was asking all the questions, but I needed to know who was answering them.

I wrote the entire book over eleven days, finishing in May 2012. It had no structure, no title, no table of contents, and certainly not a written synopsis. After those eleven days I took a week off. It was at this point that I began to question, who was my friend?

At first I thought my friend was God. Then I thought my friend was Source, a non-denominational being that was maybe God. I hired my editor, Yi Shun Lai, and as she began to edit the parables, she encouraged me to define the two characters. She suggested an exercise to draw out the mysterious storyteller. "If they are hosting separate parties, tell me what they are wearing, who they invited, what the conversation is about, and what is in each host's pockets."

Day after day, comment after comment, she kept telling me to clarify the voices, define the characters. "There is no setting, no scene, there are just voices, so they must be clear and distinct."

I didn't want to do any of it, but I did. Although it was easy for me to answer her questions about me, I struggled to do the same for my friend. "He's not wearing any clothes," I told her. "Therefore, no pockets! In fact he is not a person." *It must be God*, I thought.

But in reading the stories again, I came to the conclusion that this was not God, but my soul. I was talking to myself, but I was talking to the part of me that can tap into the source of all knowledge and wisdom, every life I have lived, every thought that is shared, every pain that is or has been felt.

There is no question that everyone can do what I did. There is nothing about me that is special or unique. In fact, I believe that many people do have dialogues with their souls but they may not share this publicly. The strange part about finding or talking to your soul is that it's not hard. Our mind makes it hard, which basically means our thoughts and belief systems make it hard. I can assure you that once you begin to experience what I experienced, an entire new world opens up, and it is filled with miracles.

There were many confirmations, signs, and wonders to guide me through the creation of this book. One came in designing the cover. It was past midnight, and I was sitting by my pool as I have done nearly every day for seven years. I stared at the stars thinking about the chosen design when I asked my soul if this was a good cover. At that very moment something happened that has never happened before in my back yard. A goose flew over my head, honking loudly. I ran inside and picked up *Animal Speak* by Ted Andrews, a book that deciphers animal symbolism. It said, among other things, that geese are signs of communication through stories and parables, they symbolize writing and great spiritual quests, and their quill is used for writing. I kept the quill on the book cover.

Another sign came when I was tired of Yi Shun challenging me. It was late at night, and I was reading her comments. Just as I said to myself, "I can do this myself," my phone turned itself on, the screen went blue, said, "Voice Control," and played a visual representation of sound waves going back and forth. "Oh," I said out loud, "I see you are telling me I do need Yi Shun. Thank you for the help, I am deeply grateful." Just to be sure, I followed up with a kind email to Yi Shun, thanking her for the wonderful help and guidance she was providing.

A third sign occurred when Yi Shun and I were discussing a story that is now an outtake. The question was "What is Truth?" I really liked that story, but Yi Shun suggested that perhaps it is best to allow all of you, the readers, to determine for yourselves what is true or not true. After all, that was the essence of what I wrote, that truth is in the eye of the beholder. After our call I went to put my dirty dishes into the kitchen sink. It was empty except for one tall wine glass. Just as I was putting the dish into the sink, I was thinking about truth. My exact thought was, "Perhaps I should allow the reader to determine the truth for themselves." At that very moment, the wine glass fell over and the stem shattered. I know from my experiences that a glass represents transparency into the non-physical realm. Its breaking meant that I had shattered an illusion.

I felt a deep sense of peace and tranquility. I immediately said a prayer, thanking God, Source, or whatever you call this omnipotent being. As I prayed, I realized the illusion that was shattered; my mind wanted to tell you the story on truth. The illusion was that this story was not for you, it was for me. I had to discover the truth for myself, just as you need to discover it for yourself. That is the essence of the story; you are the master of your ship, the captain of your vessel. What is true for you is more important than what anyone else has to say, including me. I deleted the story and inserted a short message with a blank, white page for you to contemplate your own truth.

Perhaps the most shocking revelation was the story about the atheist paradox. After reading what I had written, I realized that this story was about me. I was the one who had spent a decade trying to prove the existence of God through science. To say I was shocked is an understatement. At what point in my life did I lose my faith? Why was my mind denying all the signs and communications? Needless to say, I cried, and they were tears of joy; my faith was restored.

The final sign from God came when I was writing the Day Eleven parables. As I was trying to edit them I was getting confused and frustrated. I stopped, hopped in my car, and drove to the gas station to fill the tank and clear my mind. As the gas was pumping I sat down on the curb thinking about the definition of a day, what is time, and what is the best way to end this story. Just then a man down on his luck came up to me and asked if he could borrow two dollars. I don't normally give money to homeless people, but for some reason I did. After he took the money he started to walk away, stopped, turned around and asked, "Why are you sitting here so late at night?" I said that I was thinking. He scratched his head and replied, "You need to stop thinking so much. It's not good for you," and turned and left. I burst into laughter, got up, and went back to my car, thanking God once again for a message. Stop thinking about it—*what you wrote the first time is what I want you to say*—was the message, and so it remains as it was first written.

This is the way the story unfolded. This is the truth of how it was written. This is the light that came on inside me. This epilogue was not something I had intended to write, but because of the amazing signs and wonders from God I am compelled to share these closing stories and the peace that filled my soul.

We the people find ourselves at a once-in-a-lifetime tipping point, a dramatic awakening. A shift is occurring for humanity, and it is divinely ordained. It is a time when the people must unite and speak out so that all sides understand we must leave behind selfish desires from the World of Form.

From the Creator's point of view, never before in the history of humanity have so many needed so much, or so few controlled so many. The lovely corollary is this: Never before have so many known so much or been so enlightened. What is transparent to the transcended are the ideas that created and perpetuated a false reality, a false reality that previously sustained repressive environments. In the process of enlightenment, the transcended have shattered the preconceptions that long ago created a disturbance among men and women. We have become conscious of what binds us.

It is not so much that we as a race or nation must *decide* to consent to this point, but rather that we *declare* what is already obvious to the many and unseen by a few. We the people therefore declare on every corner of the earth, in every home and industry, that the ties that bind are far greater than what separates us. We hereby acknowledge that the color of our skin, national origin, political party, religious affiliation, or gender are of no matter to a supreme Creator and therefore ought not matter to man or institution. In the process, humanity and the citizens of every nation may accurately and boldly, if not without hazard, cast aside the illusions and disturbances that perpetuate separation.

Consider that the world has entered a new age of interdependency, where energy, food, water, and commerce are unaware of national borders established by outdated and faulty programs. Just as the essence of an individual is the summation of his principles and actions, so is a nation and a world the aggregate of our collective intentions and thoughts.

It is in this vein that the Preface was written. Each of us must choose. Will it be toys or nature, self or the many, today or tomorrow, gratification or satisfaction? My journey through eleven days in May is a love story between whom and what I love more. I declare that I love my children, family, nation, values, and Creator more than Wall Street or Madison Avenue. The conflict we now face is between God, man, and nature. A revolution has begun in silence, in no-place and in no-time. The senseless consumption, mindless addictions, and abuse of the many will end. Where, how, and when it ends is up to us to decide.

It is my deepest hope that you will discover the way of your soul, your purpose for being here, and the light that resides deep inside of you. When you do, the attachments in your life, the World of Form, and the outdated programs and beliefs will become visible. You may experience many of the emotions and bouts of suffering that I experienced, but know this: Suffering is optional. The programs don't want you to uninstall them, but you have the power to hit the delete button and send those viruses back to the trash bin where they belong. When this happens, I promise you one thing, you will find more peace, happiness, abundance, and tranquility than you have ever experienced...and you, in turn, will pass those on to others.

AUM, OM, AMEN.

FOR THE SCIENTIFICALLY INCLINED

There are many prominent theorists and theories that substantiate the metaphysical phenomena described in this book. As I learned from Thomas Kuhn in *The Structure of Scientific Revolutions,* all great theories and discoveries are initially ridiculed. I learned the same principle applies when it comes to companies that innovate—Amazon comes to mind. Both innovative theorists and corporate visionaries are ridiculed because they shatter paradigms and upset the status quo.

However, contrary to popular belief, industrial evolution—the nature by which industries and companies evolve—and science have something in common: Their stages of growth are not a series of steady and small developments, but rather a series of incremental changes followed by radical shifts that blow apart old beliefs and structures. To understand the visionaries that led these technological revolutions, all one needs to do is reflect upon the likes of Steve Jobs (Apple), Jeff Bezos (Amazon), or Bill Gates (Microsoft); just about everyone who knew them when they began their quest would tell you that these people were iconoclastic. I have been called crazy about four times in my life, and each time it was the precursor to an idea that had a growth chart that went straight up.

We are living in times where the essence of life, living, industries, nations, and yes, science and religion are about to be turned upside down and inside out. These are not normal times; it is not normal for the world to be insolvent; it is not normal for the world to have political and social revolutions on every continent; it is not normal for there to be record-breaking floods, hurricanes, earthquakes, tsunamis, tornadoes, and fires—all in the same year.

There are so many inconsistencies in modern science—anomalies—observations that don't fit our "laws." Very few people have the confidence, courage, and drive to step out in front of the pack and challenge them. Fortunately, in the realm of science, at least one man does possess these qualities. I had the privilege of meeting him a few weeks after completing *11 Days in May.*

I was having breakfast in New York City with my agent, Bill Gladstone, and philosopher-scientist-author Ervin Laszlo. It was the first time I had met Dr. Laszlo and, in preparation for our meeting, I began reading his most recent book, *BIRTH OF THE AKASHA PARADIGM: The Rediscovery of Wholeness in Cosmos and Consciousness.* This new work is the culmination of over forty years of writing and research by one of the world's greatest minds. It is in this vein that I strongly endorse this book for the scientifically inclined.

I will not attempt to summarize what Dr. Laszlo has so beautifully articulated, but rather state my case on why every scientist should not only read his book, but act on it. This new "ology" can help us understand the essence of a miracle, the power of our minds to manifest reality, and the ability of our supercomputer to visualize future events. There is a new world of unlimited potential at our fingertips, and Dr. Laszlo is on the cutting edge. If humanity fails to explore this new "ology," it risks sharing the same fate as the corporate titans that ignored technological innovations. We knew them as Blockbuster, Polaroid and Borders.

About the Author

JD Messinger is a modern day visionary whose credentials are reminiscent of a renaissance man. As a child, JD was fascinated with chemistry, electricity, and mechanics, often dismantling household appliances to decipher their operational secrets. He began his adult life as a fireman and moved on to be the former CEO of Ernst & Young Consulting, Singapore, one of 37 Distinguished Graduates from the United States Naval Academy class of 1981, a former nuclear submarine officer, and the Exxon executive who helped supervise the Valdez Oil spill cleanup. JD has a dynamic presence in the media as the creator and host of both a television show and CNN radio show. In the business world he has been an advisor to Fortune 100 clients, governments, and members of parliament on five continents.

JD was the IT person of the week for Channel News Asia and nominated for CEO of the year by CNBC Asia. Later in life, he became a Knight of Honor in the Order of St. John and received numerous corporate presidential and national awards. An international speaker, JD has been interviewed on dozens of television shows as a featured expert on innovation, crisis response, and the future of energy.

Dignitaries and executives around the world have praised his position papers, which have been distributed to numerous Presidential candidates, members of parliament, prime ministers, and royal family members in both the United States and abroad. JD has been married to Marianne for thirty years, and they are blessed with three children. The family is currently living in Texas. He is conversational in Mandarin Chinese, and in his free time he enjoys all things adventurous such as fencing, boxing, scuba diving, hiking, and hosting talk radio.